Foreword

BY MIKE TRIMBY

John 'Moon Eyes' Cooper at Cadwell Park
(Mortons Archive)

Mike Trimby
(Mortons Archive)

Memories can be very strange. I first became aware of John Cooper at the age of about 13 or 14 and I can never think of those times without remembering the taste of ham sandwiches tainted with the smell of petrol.

My parents were divorced and I spent every weekend with my dad at his home in Frome. Whenever possible we would ride off on his 197cc James to a motorcycle event. We went to scrambles, grass tracks and trials but my preferred outings were to the road races at Thruxton or Castle Combe. There we would position ourselves at a favourite corner, Quarry Bends at Castle Combe, and eat our ham sandwiches which had travelled to the event packed next to, and contaminated by, the ever-present can of fuel which Dad always carried for emergency use.

It was at Castle Combe that I first witnessed the brilliance of John Cooper on a Manx Norton wearing his moon eyes helmet. After the races we would visit the paddock, completely open in those days, and pester the riders, especially John, for autographs.

It was those early outings and the influence of heroes like John that motivated me to have a go at road racing myself and this started me on a lifelong career in the sport which eventually led to my current role in IRTA. During that career I have been lucky enough to meet and work with some of the greats like Hailwood and Agostini who, despite all the hype about modern stars, are in my eyes still the best of all time.

My position also allowed me to meet and eventually become a friend of John Cooper and to me, John was a revelation. Here was a man I once idolised, who had achieved so much in racing but remarkably was a genuinely nice bloke with no airs or graces.

As I have got to know John better and learnt things from other people I have been made aware of his generous nature. Even today, when most people of his age are taking things easy, John is always there to offer help when needed. I know he has often assisted racing people and others financially, and sometimes this has never been acknowledged. But John never complains or changes his ways.

Living in the Isle of Man I don't get to see John and his lovely wife Rosie as often as I would like. Usually we meet at The British GP and sometimes at the San Marino event. However, I was really honoured when John visited the Island a few years ago and was good enough to invite me to a dinner with Geoff Duke.

My dad would have been so proud!

Contents

Pushing away at the start of the 350cc race, Scarborough International, September, 1963. John Cooper on the far right (Unknown)

MOON EYES

John Cooper

THE MAN WHO BEAT AGO

CONTENTS

Editor:
Richard Skelton

Production editor:
Pauline Hawkins

Designer:
Craig Lamb, Kriele Ltd
design_lamb@btinternet.com

Cover design:
Mike Baumber

Publisher:
Steve O'Hara

Publishing director:
Dan Savage

Commercial director:
Nigel Hole

Marketing manager:
Charlotte Park
cpark@mortons.co.uk

Advertising manager:
Billy Manning

Printed by:
William Gibbons and Sons

ISBN:
978-1-911276-95-1

Introduction

BY CHRIS CARTER Motorcycling author and journalist

Cooperman on the BSA Rocket 3
(Mortons Archive)

Chris Carter
(Unknown)

The Carter family knew John Cooper long before he became a road racing superstar. After the war my father, Reg Carter, kept his motorcycles and a Morgan three-wheeler in a lock-up opposite Billy Wilson Butchers on Windmill Lane, in Derby.

The Coopers lived nearby and John, like me, still a schoolboy then of course, was employed by Billy to deliver meat to his regular customers. I got to know John well and even helped him out on his round.

More about that later. Young John was a member of the Derby Phoenix Motorcycle Club and so was my dad and my brother, Brian, who was a talented artist. On club nights, Brian and John would sit at the back of the pub room, giggling away at mildly irreverent cartoons and caricatures produced by my brother. Club officials tried hard, but in vain, to control them.

But before all this, the Carter family had been well known to a certain Mr Alec Crone of Ashbourne, the father of John's future wife, Rosemary. For a number of years Grandma Carter and my Auntie Ruth ran Carter's Cafe overlooking the Market Place in Ashbourne.

During the Second World War the cafe, like all such businesses, operated under strict food rationing and Alec kept a few pigs on some land near Sandybrook Hall. Now the Carters needed pork, while Mr Crone was keen on any sugar, coffee and butter that might be going spare. A deal was done and a regular arrangement was established. All on the black market, of course, but needs must!

This special publication tells the story of John 'Moon Eyes' Cooper... the down-to-earth Derbyshire lad who beat Italian world champion Giacomo Agostini to take top spot at the 1971 Race of the Year at Mallory Park.

In his own words, Cooperman tells of the bikes, the races, the riding style, the rivals... and how, even without a factory ride, he beat the best in the world to cement a place in motorcycling history.

Interspersed with tributes from colleagues, friends and fellow riders, this is a fascinating insight into the world of competitive motorcycle racing in the 1950s, 60s and 70s – an era many would say were the halcyon days of the sport – and is peppered with rarely seen images from the Cooper family's own collection as well as the respected and comprehensive Mortons archive.

Quiet concentration. Warming up the 500 Seeley, Mallory Park, 1972 (Jan Burgers)

CHILDHOOD & TEENAGE YEARS

I was born in January 1938 and living during the war wasn't easy. I can remember the sirens going then and hiding under the stairs or running down the street to get into an air raid shelter. I can remember the Jerries going over, the searchlights and bombs raining down. It was a nerve-racking time.

We didn't have enough coal in the winter, and we had to save our coupons for a pair of shoes or a shirt, and I can remember swapping coupons for things because we had no money. Even after the war we still had our ration books for years and years. Then later things started to get a bit easier and when I came out of the army in 1958 I could see a future when everybody had a car. It happened eventually, but for years everyone had to save up for things. A washing machine, a TV, although they were usually rented, or on the never-never.

Our first TV only had a nine-inch screen. We had to watch it in the dark and after a while we bought a magnifying glass to stand in front of it. Programmes were only broadcast a few hours a day and there were frequent breaks in transmission when a caption would come up saying normal service will be resumed in half an hour so we'd go off and make a cup of tea. Then we'd come back and put all the lights out again and carry on watching.

Toddler John finding his feet
(Cooper Collection)

My dad was a slaughterman originally at the Co-op in Woods Lane in Derby and when I was about 12 or 13 I had to go down there on my pushbike and take him his lunch and watch him killing pigs and sheep, which was horrible really.

And as you well recall, Chris, I was a butcher's boy and one day I was delivering to an eccentric old lady called Mrs Johnson in Piper Street and she'd had a fit or a seizure or something and when I got there she was lying on the floor, twitching. It frightened me so much that from then on I used to give you sixpence to deliver her meat!

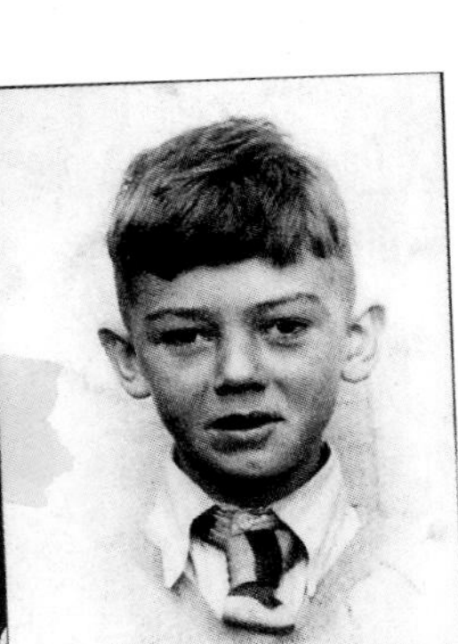

Schoolboy John
(Cooper Collection)

LEFT: **Testing out lean angles. With dad Phil, mum Joan and sister Ann**
(Cooper Collection)

Chris Carter: **Yes, I remember it well. I like to say it's the only time I've been braver than a British champion! How did you get into motorcycling?**

I had a bicycle as a kid and I was keen on cleaning it and looking after it and I was always interested in motorbikes. My dad had an old motorcycle which he left leaning up in the yard and I remember when I was about eight I used to get a lift from your dad in his BSA Sloper sidecar outfit and I used to ride along standing on the seat looking over the screen. That wouldn't be allowed today.

Then, when I was about 11 or 12, not long after the war, there was a lad down the street who had a 250 BSA and he used to kick this bike up and ride it up and down. I used to stand on the corner of Westleigh Avenue where I lived and hope he'd ask me if I wanted a go on the back. Occasionally he did and I'd jump on. Petrol was on ration so he couldn't take me far but he'd take me up the main road, Kingsway, and back.

Around the same time I had a job helping on a farm. I used to ride my bicycle out into the countryside to Chaddesden village to help a chap milk his cows and other odd jobs and he had an old Matchless motorbike. He said you can have that if you like, so me and my pal Trevor Hartland – he was a nice lad, lived opposite – walked there together one Sunday morning and we pushed it all the way home to Derby. It was easily eight miles, and don't forget I was only about 12 or 13 and very small and slight because after the war you didn't get a lot of food.

Anyway, we got it going and then we pushed it all the way back to Chaddesden again and from then on I used to ride it round the fields, up and down and round and about until the farmer got so fed up with me he backed his tractor into it accidentally on purpose and that was the end of that.

I took any opportunity to have a go on a bike. When I was about 14 I went along to the RAC/ACU Training Scheme and they used to let me ride a BSA Bantam and a 350 Ariel up and down a long drive at Hopwell Park, and Tom Smith the woodwork teacher at school was interested in bikes and he let me ride his Royal Enfield up and down another private drive.

Then when I left school at 15 in 1953, I got a full-time job as a mechanic at Wilemans Motorcycles in Derby. My dad knew Bernard Wileman, who was a really nice chap, and he agreed to give me an interview. I caught the bus down to Wilemans and spoke to his brother Ken. He could see I was keen and took me on there and then. My first job was to gunk second-hand bikes down and clean them ready to go in the shop, and from there I went on to learn the motorbike trade. The Wilemans were very good to me really.

With Chris Carter's dad, Reg
(Chris Carter)

On the farm
(Cooper Collection)

Chris Carter: What about competitive motorcycling?

I was always interested in racing. I went to watch grass track at Mallory Park. It was just a very fast grass oval. They ran the sidecars right-handed, the way the track runs now, and the solos left-handed. I saw Bill Boddice and others there. It was absolutely flat out and sometimes the outfits would get out of control and smash through the wooden fencing. Then of course Clive Wormleighton bought it and turned it into a road racing track.

A local racer called Roy Caygill had a Grand Prix Triumph and a Velocette KTT. He used to work in the bodyshop on the railway and I used to stand outside waiting for him to go by after work, promenading up and down. And there was a guy called Ted Goodwin who used to ride in the Manx every year. I helped him prepare his bike for the Manx Grand Prix and he wanted to sell me his James trials bike. I knew it was immaculate because I'd worked on it with him, but my dad said no, you've got to buy a new bike. So I bought a brand new James Commando on hire purchase and I used to ride in trials and the odd standard tyre race at scramble meetings at Clifton and Turnditch.

My first-ever trial was at Bradley. I was only 16 and I was ready to go off and feeling a bit nervous. Jeff Shaw, who worked at the BSA factory, very kindly said to me: "Don't worry about it lad, you'll be fine. You're young enough to be the next Jeff Smith." Well, I never did become a really good trials and scrambles rider like Jeff but I think it's fair to say I did all right at road racing.

Half the trouble was I was very light, which was good for road racing, but in trials I kept getting wheel-spin. On a trial we'd all put about 4lb in the back tyre, and about 6lb in the front but I was so light I should've been putting 2lb in the back and 4lb in the front. Of course, nobody helped me out by telling me that. I can remember once trying to go down a steep hill called Lumb Lane, slithering around and having one hell of a job, and then Norman Storer rode up the hill and passed me with his feet up.

Norman was a great all-rounder and later on we had a few good races together on the roads. One time at Aberdare Park we touched and he went over the handlebars, making a right mess of himself. It was just one of those things and we're still friends today.

Scrambling was incredibly physical and the top riders were big, strong guys on very good bikes and I was too small and slight to compete really. I once had a ride on John Griffiths' works Greeves at Clifton but late in the race I was so tired when I got halfway down the straight and came to the jump I couldn't shut off and

Competing in the 1955 Bemrose Trophy trial on a 125cc Francis Barnett (at Hawk's Nest, Birchover)
(Cooper Collection)

I flew up into the trees. And scrambling just didn't appeal to me as much as road racing. Sometimes you can do things well and sometimes you can't, and I found out that road racing was something I could do to a good standard, and that it was the type of motorcycling that I enjoyed most of all.

Weavers Hill scramble, 1956
(Cooper Collection)

LEFT: Scrambling at Clifton, 1960
(Cooper Collection)

Chris Carter: How did you get into road racing?

I was in the Pathfinders Club and when I was 16 I used to go up to Osmaston Manor with a chap called Tom Pratley and help knock the posts in and hang the ropes to mark out the viewing areas before scrambles meetings. Then I watched my first road racing there and I thought to myself, I wouldn't mind a go at this, it looks pretty easy to me.

So I got some tyres off a bloke called Don Whelan who used to do continental racing, fitted a high compression cylinder head on my James, put a straight-through exhaust on it, and made a little air scoop for the front brake.

I was basically just copying the things other people were doing, guys like Barry Rogers and Roy Robinson, and it was all very amateurish. On the day I was very nervous but once the flag dropped I was fine, and first time out I won the 200cc heat, and then I led the final from start to finish. I won eight quid. Good money in those days!

But it was a bit of a fluke really, purely because I was so small and light. I only weighed about seven stone, and the second and third place people were Molly Briggs and Doug Allen and they were a lot bigger and heavier than me, so on my little James I had an advantage.

A bygone era. Osmaston Manor paddock, early 1950s
(Mark Weston)

John on the James. After winning his first ever road race at Osmaston Manor, 1955, aged 17
(Cooper Collection)

Suited and booted. John outside the family home wearing leathers borrowed from Bill Lomas
(Cooper Collection)

The track at Osmaston Manor was only about 10ft wide with trees everywhere. The most dangerous section of all was even narrower and they made that a no-passing zone. I was there recently attending the Ashbourne Show and I was standing at what had been the first corner. I said to the car park attendant: "Do you know, when I used to race motorcycles here as a kid, this was the first bend on the track," and he said: "Oh no mate, this was never a race track." "Yes it was," I said. "Oh no, no," he said. "You're thinking of Oulton Park." You can't tell some people.

International privateer Peter Ferbrache would come up from London to race at Osmaston Manor and at our other local track, Alton Towers. He'd give our local stars a run for their money, people like Freddie Wallis and Alf Briggs.

Alf was one of the top motorbike racers in the East Midlands in the 50s and the early 60s despite being terribly short-sighted, which may have played a part in him having some horrible accidents! Alf used to ride in scrambles as well as being a road racer and he rode with high handlebars. His wife Molly Briggs used to ride in the ISDT and the Scottish Six Day Trial and she did a bit of scrambling and road racing, and she was a good little rider too.

So I'd made a bit of a start racing motorbikes as a teenager but when I came back from watching the TT at the Isle of Man in 1956 with my pals Barry Rogers and Keith Chapman, my National Service call-up papers had arrived. I had to leave Wilemans and the Derbyshire motorcycling scene and do two years in the forces.

LEFT: John Cooper with Alf and Rosemary Briggs and David Burrell, paddock, Kirkcaldy, 1958
(Cooper Collection)

Last days of freedom. With Pete Minion and his 500cc BSA Gold Star at the 1956 Isle of Man TT
(Cooper Collection)

YOU'RE IN THE ARMY NOW!

I was enlisted in the army and I had to report to Aldershot in Kent for basic training. I got the train down. It was a long journey by rail and then I had to walk about two miles to Ramillies Barracks. When I got there I was feeling pretty shattered and I received a rude introduction to army life which I'll never forget. I'd no sooner passed through the perimeter gate when a Sergeant Major screamed out: "Get off that f*****g grass!"

And I'd only been there an hour when we all had to have a haircut. The barber said to everybody: "How do you want it?" but it was just his little joke because no matter what you said he just went straight over the top with his clippers. He scalped us all. Next they took away all our civilian clothes and gave us our uniforms and that was it. We were in the army.

Before long they told us all what specialist training we would receive and, of all the damn silly things, I had to go into the catering corps. After basic training I went to the cookery instruction centre to do six months' cookery training before being posted. I wasn't best pleased at first but it turned out to be a good thing because I learned to cook to a good standard and I ended up assigned to the officers' mess at Sennybridge Training Camp in South Wales. I had a good diet including fillet steak and chips on a regular basis and in two years I grew about six inches and put on two stone. When I'd first turned up at Aldershot I'd only just been tall enough to get in.

My friend Norman Storer was in the army trials team and there were some other motorbike people in the forces but I didn't come across them. I had a Tiger 90 Triumph and a 350 Ariel while I was in that I used to get about on, but the job meant I often had to work weekends so I hardly had any opportunities to get away to race. In fact I didn't have much to do with motorcycling at all while I was doing my national service, so I was out of it for two years really.

But there were some exceptions. I rode a James for Bill Lomas's dad Harry and then I had an outing on the Royal Enfield that Bill had raced at the Manx Grand Prix. Bill Lomas was a successful grand prix rider at the time and a little bit big-headed. He considered himself a bit of a Mr Big and he was picky about who he'd speak to and that included me, but I got on very well with his dad and his mother, Annie.

One day Harry asked me to ride the Lomas James at Alton Towers and Mallory Park so I did that and then he asked me if I'd like to have a go on Bill's ex-Manx Grand Prix Royal Enfield. I did okay in a qualifying heat but in the final the piston melted and Harry said: "I don't understand it. Alf Briggs has ridden this bike and Peter Tomes, and they never had any trouble." I said: "That's all well and good, but they obviously didn't go very fast on it, did they?" The truth was, the bike had had its day. It was outdated and I didn't ride it again. Years later I became very friendly with Bill Lomas. Towards the end of his life he was a much nicer person and I used to go and see him once a week and sit with him and have a cup of tea. In the end he got Alzheimer's, which was sad but I think it was good for him to talk about the old days.

Get some in! National Service, Aldershot Barracks, aged 18
Cooper Collection)

BACK IN CIVVY STREET

When I came out of the army in 1958 I went back to work at Wilemans. I wanted to get back into racing but I had no money and Ken Wileman gave me a damaged James Captain frame. I straightened it up and advertised for a Triumph Tiger Cub engine. I bought two and I put the best one in the frame and then I bought a decent pair of forks, a nice front brake and a Triumph back wheel. Molly Briggs gave me a front wheel and I put it all together and built a Cub Special ready for the 1959 season. And when it was

John in action at Aintree in 1959 on his Triumph Cub Special
(Cooper Collection)

Mallory Park hairpin, 1960. John Cooper (James Club) inside Percy Tait (Brearley Cub)
(Cooper Collection)

done I went down a side road near where I lived and tested it by flying up and down awhile, making sure I cleared off home before anyone complained and a policeman came.

Later I had a 350cc BSA special which I obtained from the Minion brothers, another motorcycle-dealing family in Derby. Bob Minion was the father of the family and he started the firm in 1925. By the mid-1950s it was being run by his sons Lionel, Peter and Rob. Peter used to race a Norton and then he had a Gold Star which he rode in Clubmans TTs in the mid-1950s. I went along with the family the year I was called up. Peter's brother Rob used to be the mechanic at Minions and at some point he had got hold of a Manx Norton rolling chassis after its engine had been sold for 500cc car racing. He put a 350cc Gold Star engine in it for Peter to race and eventually that bike was bought for me to race by a chap called Russ Warren.

In the end I left Wilemans and went to work for the Minion family instead because they were always very supportive of my ideas about racing. The Wilemans were never particularly interested; in fact, I once asked them if I could have time off to ride at Scarborough. They agreed reluctantly and Ken scornfully said: "Who do you think you are, John Surtees?" Anyway, I won the 350cc final which of course was reported in the papers. Nothing was ever said about it afterwards. It was never acknowledged.

The silly thing was, I earned more money that weekend than I'd get in two months at Wilemans. I won about £60 and I was only getting about £7 a week at Wilemans at the time, and the foreman there was only on £8.10s a week. Mind you, I thought that was a fortune. I thought, how can anybody spend £8.10s a week? A haircut was about 6d and a pint of beer was a shilling back then.

NSU Quicklys on tour. Fun and games with the Minion family on Skegness beach, John aboard PCH 297
(Cooper Collection)

Cadwell Park, 1959. Cresting the Mountain on the James Captain/Triumph Cub Special
(Cooper Collection)

Chris Carter: You always went well at Mallory Park, a circuit which you later became associated with very strongly, but this was the time when you started travelling further afield to race. You mention Scarborough, where else did you go?

I rode at Cadwell Park on my Triumph Cub and Peter Middleton was there riding a 500cc Norton. In practice we got down to the bottom of the mountain and I passed Peter there and held him off until he re-passed me on the start-finish on his Norton.

When he got back into the paddock he said to his brother: "Who's that youth wearing a red hat on that Triumph Cub?" His brother looked in the programme and said: "It's a lad called Cooper." Peter then said: "I hope he never gets a good bike!"

SIXTIES SCENE

Chris Carter: Russ Warren was your entrant for a long time in the early 1960s. How did that relationship come about?

John Cooper in action, 350cc BSA-Norton, Cadwell Park, 1959
(Cooper Collection)

At the end of the 1950s I was riding my Triumph Cub and an Anzani Special owned by Maurice Patey. Maurice worked at Ingles, the BSA agents, and he went on to become joint founder of Silk Motorcycles. One day a racer called Peter Tomes came into Wilemans and I asked him when he was riding next. He said he'd had a crash at Scarborough and decided enough was enough, he was calling it a day. He told me his bikes belonged to a chap called Russ Warren, the manager of Wraggs Motorcycles in Sheffield. You want to give him a ring, he said, and see if he'll lend them to you.

I rang Russ up and arranged to meet him the following weekend at Mallory Park where I was riding my Cub. He said he had a 500cc BSA Gold Star in bits which he'd lent to a chap called Harry Hutchinson, who owned a pub in Birchover. Russ said if I went and fetched it and built it back up I could borrow it.

Well, when I went to fetch it, it was literally a heap of parts piled up in a chicken run. The bike was completely broken down and some of it was missing but I put it all back together and took it to Mallory Park for the Race of the Year. I finished well down because the bike was outclassed by Nortons, and there were some big stars there, including John Surtees on his MV. But I qualified on it and finished tenth or twelfth or something in the main race and Russ let me carry on using it. I rode the 500 Gold Star for a year and did quite well on it.

During that year Russ bought me a 350 Gold Star special in a Manx frame from the Minion brothers, and a bit later in 1961 he sold both those bikes and bought

On the BSA-Norton at Cadwell Park,1960
(Cooper Collection)

In action at Cadwell Park (1959) and Mallory Park (1960) on the Russ Warren 500cc BSA Gold Star
(Cooper Collection)

a 350cc Norton from Fred Rutherford in London. It had supposedly been tuned by Bill Lacey and when I first got it I was really excited because I thought Nortons were the be all and end all at the time. But it wasn't as fast as the Gold Star and for two meetings I really struggled on it. I couldn't do anything with it and I was finishing well downfield, but Rob Minion did some research and we found out the valve timing on my bike was absolutely miles out.

After I put the timing right the first meeting was at Cadwell Park and the star man that day was another chap from Derbyshire, John Hartle. Well, we set off and before long I was right behind John and I soon realised I could pass him easily. The bike was flying but because it was John Hartle up ahead I thought I'd better

Flying on the Norton. September 1961, Cadwell Park. The first of many great photographs of John Cooper in this book by the great 'Nick' Nicholls
(Nick Nicholls Collection, Mortons Archive)

LEFT: **On the 350 BSA-Norton at Scarborough in 1960, battling with Ron Cousins (350 Norton)**
(Cooper Collection)

not push my luck and I stayed behind him and finished second. After that I went really well on that 350, and then Russ bought a 500cc Norton for me from Dennis Pratt. That was a good bike too so I had two competitive bikes and I did quite well on them for a number of years.

That 350 Norton was a good 'un but unfortunately an engineer called Frank Platt, who was well known around Derby, had an idea for improving it which had the opposite effect. He used to make parts and he said to me one day: "I've just been looking at Dan Shorey's bike and I've noticed it's got a 500 carburettor on it. If you bring yours round I'll bore your inlet out for you and put a big carb on for you." Well, it wrecked it. It was never any good after that. Very ordinary. With the small carburettor it had good acceleration and it was only very slightly down on top speed, perfect for places like Scarborough.

Chris Carter: You were particularly successful at Scarborough during that period, I recall. What was the circuit like?

I won 14 international races at Scarborough, and I broke the 500cc lap record which Geoff Duke had set on the Gilera and which had stood for years.

The track was very bumpy, very narrow, and extremely dangerous, but it didn't really bother me too much because I started my career riding in trials and scrambles, and road racing at Osmaston Manor, which was lined with trees. So I was like Norman Storer in that I was used to rough going and flying over bumps, and road racing was a lot easier than scrambling as far as I was concerned.

Early Scarborough

At Scarborough, June 1963, John scored a win and a second on this day
(Mortons Archive)

Fuelling up
(Starlight Studios, Scarborough)

RIGHT: **On the start-line, early 1960s**
(Nick Nicholls Collection, Mortons Archive)

John garlanded after winning a 350cc race at Scarborough in 1961, with Russ and Madge Warren
(Cooper Collection)

Bigger and better things. Scarborough, September 1961
(Nick Nicholls Collection, Mortons Archive)

DEAD
ENGINES
72
69
56
56
49
46
53
53
47

Royal Enfield roll call (from left): Griff Jenkins, John Cooper, Charles Mortimer Snr, Jack Booker, Leo Davenport and Geoff Duke
(Mortons Archive)

Chris Carter: So did Russ or Wraggs prepare the bikes for you? What were the financial arrangements?

Russ Warren bought the bikes, but I maintained them and paid all the travelling costs etc., and I used to give Russ half my prize money.

I always paid my dues because I never wanted to end up having to stop motorbike racing. Because the tax man was on to me for some back taxes, I ended up paying his tax as well as my own. I got half the prize money but paid the tax on the whole bloody lot.

I had some good times with Russ but in the end, because I had to pay all the expenses, I didn't make much money and in the mid-Sixties I bought the bikes off him and went private and I was a privateer for pretty much the whole of my career from then on.

GENTLEMAN GEOFF

I rode for Geoff Duke for a short time in the early 1960s when he was team manager for Royal Enfield. Not too many years before this, Geoff had been a famous grand prix rider, and a multiple world champion of course, so it was quite something to get a telegram from him. But unfortunately the offer was to ride a new 250cc Royal Enfield, not one of his world championship-winning Gileras.

He asked me if I'd ride the new bike at Silverstone and in the Isle of Man. It wasn't a great machine to be honest, not very fast, but at Silverstone I managed to set a lap record for a 250cc production bike at the time.

Geoff Duke was really nice fellow and excellent company. A few years ago when I was going over at the TT I rang him up and invited him and his wife Daisy out to dinner. Steve Parrish and Mike Trimby ended up coming along and it was a very pleasant dinner party indeed. I really enjoyed the evening and so did my wife, Rosemary, who found him particularly charming.

He was always a bit of a ladies' man. When we were at Silverstone with Royal Enfield he turned up with a black eye, and the story was someone had given him a good hiding.

He was apparently having a bit of a fling with the wife of a Worcestershire cricketer at the time and one day this chap had gone off on the bus to play cricket and Geoff nipped round to his house.

But the cricketer got his foot caught in the door of the bus, came home early and found Geoff with his missus. The chap hit Geoff for six!

MOON EYES

Chris Carter: You're famous for having Moon Eyes on your racing helmets and the idea has been copied around the world. How did it come about?

There was a lad who used to come into Minions when I was there who was a bit of an artist and he painted Jiminy Cricket on a couple of my crash helmets, JC being my initials. But when I had an accident and needed another helmet doing in a hurry he was ill and couldn't do it. So I put some Moon Eyes stickers on instead and ended up sticking with them. The name Moon Eyes came originally from Dean Moon, a California hot-rod builder and speed shop owner.

From a commentating and spectating point of view they were highly distinctive and made it easy for people to spot me. Nowadays the riders all have fancy and elaborate designs but from a distance, at the speed they're travelling, you often can't tell one from another and they don't really mean anything.

The eyes have it! John Cooper leading Derek Minter, Snetterton, July 1964
(Nick Nicholls Collection, Mortons Archive)

Chris Carter: And some fans started putting Moon Eyes on their crash helmets as well because John Cooper was a very popular person on the racing scene in Britain, and part of that was because he was a down-to-earth and approachable Derbyshire man who spoke without airs and graces.

Early Sixties

An early encounter with Mike Hailwood, Aberdare Park, August 1961
(Nick Nicholls Collection, Mortons Archive)

RIGHT: **Getting to grips with the 500 Manx Norton at Cadwell Park**
(Mortons Archive)

Keeping the front down on the 350 Norton at Cadwell Park, September 1964
(Nick Nicholls Collection, Mortons Archive

Another winning ride, May 1964
(Mortons Archive)

Hammer down. Ambulance crew watching on
(Malcolm Carling Collection)

John 'on it' at the Elbow, Mallory Park
(Mortons Archive)

Formation flying. John Cooper (Triumph Bonneville) and Tony Melody (Norton Commando), 500 mile production race, Thruxton 1969.
(Mortons Archive)

Keeping it smooth. British Championships at Oulton Park
(Mortons Archive)

Cornering in classic John Cooper style, Oulton Park, 1966
(Malcolm Carling Collection)

KNEE OUT!

Chris Carter: As you became better known, your distinctive riding style attracted attention. You didn't stay tucked in while cornering.

I was definitely ahead of the times with my riding style and the first rider to ride with his knees out. I started that, although it can be traced back to Norman Storer originally. He used to ride a Gold Star and because the carburettor came so close to your right leg it didn't get any fresh air. So when he went into a corner he used to deliberately wave his knee out a little bit to keep it away from the carburettor. Noting this, I started doing it big style on my BSA and then I carried on with it on the Norton, around Gerards and places like that. I found it steadied the bike no end so I did it on left-handers as well.

And if you move about and hang off the bike you alter the centre of gravity and you can do that to good effect. Paul Smart said he was the first person to ride with his knee out, but I said: "Okay Paul, show me a picture taken before 1966 with you holding your knee out," and he couldn't do it.

John Cooper, 1966: **"I've touched the ground with my knee on several occasions – but I've always been off my bike at the time! My knees do get in the way sometimes, especially on narrow, winding circuits like Scarborough where they touch banks and other obstacles.'**

Double win over Phil Read and others at Mallory Park in June 1964. "John Cooper's riding style can hardly be described as the most polished in the world! But his unique technique certainly paid off at Mallory. Displaying fantastic body lean and literally hanging on by the seat of his pants, the 26-year-old Derby gents' outfitter showed all the professionals the way home."

Paul Smart gets his knee out, but John did it first!
(Unknown)

John Cooper, Mike Hailwood and Derek Minter. Close-quarters action at Brands Hatch in the 1965 Hutchinson 100
(Malcolm Carling Collection)

2

British lightweight action at Mallory Park with John Cooper (Greeves) leading Derek Minter (Cotton) (Mortons Archive)

MALCOLM WHEELER
Former racer and
editor of *Classic Racer* magazine

Can anyone remember who it was that said: "You should never meet your heroes"?

As a lad I grew up in a small Lincolnshire Wolds village within earshot of arguably the UK's finest short circuit, Cadwell Park. And boys being boys, all the lads from the village were drawn to the track and all the noise and smells created there. Long before any of us lads had even started to dream about owning our own motorcycles we cycled up to the circuit and, with our pocket money clearly not being enough to pay the entrance fee, we found a suitable hole in the hedge.

I can't remember where I left my reading glasses an hour ago, but I can remember those early meetings clearly. Once in the circuit we wandered round the open paddock and marvelled at the race bikes on open view. And every one of the leather-clad riders was held in awe. As we got braver and had a better understanding of what racing was about, we produced tatty notebooks or scraps of paper and plucked up the courage to ask for signatures. Mine are still in the attic somewhere! As my interest grew I spent more time watching trackside and, with the help of an older cousin's discarded motorcycle magazines, I could soon identify the majority of the grid. But one rider stood out from the crowd.

John Cooper had a unique style; check out the images in this great book. It was radical; long before anyone had dreamt of dragging their knee on the track John almost did. In an era when elbows in and knees on the tank was the norm, he climbed all over the bike and made it go where he wanted it to.

John won't remember I'm sure, but I plucked up the courage to talk to him in the paddock at Cadwell one day; it was around the time when his Moon Eyes first appeared on his helmet, and he made the time to talk to this spotty kid. I walked off with my chest puffed out.

As you will see in these pages, John raced against and beat the very best during his career, which I continued to follow with great interest. After John had retired from the sport, as had I after my own race career, our paths crossed regularly at shows and parade events and we always made time to chat about our shared passion. We even have similar opinions on today's racers.

Surrounded by fans after yet another win at Scarborough (Cooper Collection)

Today I'm proud to consider John a friend, and honoured to have been asked to add a few words to this long-overdue book; I can almost picture him blushing slightly as he reads this.

So who was it then that said: "You should never meet your heroes…"?

Chris Carter: By 1964 you were established as one of the top racers in the country. Who were the other 'men to beat'?

Mike Hailwood was the big star in the Sixties and you could go to Oulton Park, or Mallory Park or Brands Hatch and you could always rely on Derek Minter being very competitive, and to beat him was quite a thing. I once showed Derek Minter a photograph of the two of us, with me in the lead. He said: "You want to hang on to that picture, there's not many of them about!" There were all sorts of short-circuit specialists around, like Dave Croxford, Dan Shorey, Griff Jenkins, Joe Dunphy and George Catlin, some of them perhaps not so well known now but they were all good riders who'd give you a good race. Ken Redfern had a few good rides and won the Race of the Year, but didn't do a lot after that, and there were always people on the brink of getting somewhere.

Dan Shorey was a good little rider but he used to ride around the middle of the bloody road and block it up so he was always a difficult bloke to pass.

I remember at Oulton Park in particular I never knew where he was going to go from one lap to the next. We used to call him Banbury Dan, the quick-change artist because he used to ride a 125, 250, 350 and a 500 on the same day.

I was the bloke to beat at a lot of short circuits. Peter Williams says that. He said he was going into the Esses once at Mallory Park, sitting up and braking, and I was still accelerating while I was turning in. He said he couldn't believe how fast I could go through the Esses at Mallory.

Fast men! John Cooper and Derek Minter are Norton-mounted, with Mike Hailwood on a Tom Kirby AJS in a 350cc battle royal at Brands Hatch
(Nick Nicholls Collection, Mortons Archive)

There were a lot of good riders, and most days you couldn't say who was going to win. I can remember racing at Snetterton back in the days before the chicane, and six of us fanned out down the start-finish straight on the last lap and crossed the line together. The bikes were far more evenly matched than today with very little between them.

First lap at Mallory Park, John showing at the front as usual
(Unknown)

Testing the back-to-front Norton at Mallory Park with tuner Ray Petty on a cold day in November 1965
(Nick Nicholls Collection, Mortons Archive)

Chris Carter: Could a good tuner make a difference?

There wasn't much you could do to a 500 Norton to make it quicker than the next man's. The only way to make it win was to put a good, fast rider on it. Derek Minter's bikes were always very good but then again, so was Derek. The good tuners had good riders, so they made each other look good. If a tuner had a rider like Derek Minter, Mike Hailwood or myself, it looked good when we won or finished second or third. But the guys who finished fourth, fifth, sixth, seventh, eighth had bikes that were equally good. In fact, one day I went to Brands Hatch and my 500 packed up and Rex Butcher's dad said to me: "Would you like to borrow our Rex's spare 500? It's never been much of a bike. In fact, you can tell me what you think's up with it." Well, I set off and I was leading the race with Rex second. I thought I'd better not beat Rex, but when Derek Minter started catching us I cleared off and won and Rex had to settle for third behind Minter. After the race Rex's dad said: "I think we've identified the problem!" I felt a bit bad about that.

Francis Beart did an engine for me once or twice and Ray Petty did me some engines, but they didn't really tune them, they just put them together properly. They didn't do anything special, just got the squish clearances and the timing absolutely right and that sort of thing. They were not really any better than the ones I did myself and they charged a small fortune. I went to Oulton Park once and Francis Beart had prepared my engine. I used to rev the Norton to 7200rpm, and Francis said: "Try revving it to 7800." I tried revving it to seven-eight but it blew up, wrecking the piston and the con rod. I said: "You told me to do that and now look what's happened!"

"Oh well," he said, "that's just hard luck, isn't it?"

I spent a lot of time working on my bikes, doing my own maintenance, and they were always immaculately turned out and checked over very carefully. I think that goes a long way. A lot of people don't work on their bikes, can't even change a sprocket, whereas I would do full engine rebuilds, the lot. So yes, Ray Petty and Francis Beart would sometimes do engines for me but I don't really think it made a lot of difference. It was all in the mind.

MCN Calendar cover, 1965 shows John keeping it neat on his TT debut the previous year
(MCN)

Chris Carter: Was there a good atmosphere among the riders? Did you all get on, and did you help each other?

Was there camaraderie? Absolutely. Sitting on the backs of the trucks, talking to each other, chatting with spectators. But nowadays it's nowhere near as friendly. They lock themselves in their motorhomes or hide away in the garages. People never see them. Ron Haslam tells me even the mechanics in different teams aren't allowed to talk to one another any more. We were accessible to the fans in the paddock all the time. Years ago there weren't many places that had lock-up garages and nobody had massive motorhomes, and riders would sit on the tailgates of their vans or in their cabs and talk to the fans, and that was the way it was. I remember the first time Mike Hailwood's bikes turned up in a great big lorry, with about four bikes in the back and Jim Adams the mechanic, but Mike was always open and friendly. We were all happy to talk to the spectators and sign autographs and we didn't know any different. Paddock access was never restricted like it is now.

I never minded helping people. Other riders used to say to me, what sprockets do you use at Mallory, or whatever, and I used to tell them. Some people used to be secretive about that sort of thing but I always thought it didn't really make any difference. They could either ride a bike or they couldn't, and if you were a better rider you'd beat them anyway.

People didn't understand it when riders came over here from abroad and I'd tell them what gearing to use and what were the best lines, and a few years later when the Americans came over for the Match Races, I helped them no end; Gary Nixon, Dave Aldana and those guys.

Moon Eyes and little Bill
(Nick Nicholls Collection, Mortons Archive)

COSTS AND PRACTICALITIES

Chris Carter: What about the economics of racing?

In the Sixties, as long as you were winning fairly often it was possible to make a living as a racer, but I always had a job. I worked as a mechanic at Minions Motorcycles, then I worked for my dad, and from 1965 onwards I had a garage and filling station.

The rewards could be really good. I raced at Cadwell Park one time in 1965 and the big race of the day had a £500 prize for winning, £100 for second, £50 for third. Cadwell owner Charlie Wilkinson put a big prize fund together but all the money was loaded up at the top end. Anyway, Phil Read shot off in front on his four-cylinder 250 Yamaha which was far faster than a 500 Norton, but two laps from the end I saw a puff of smoke coming out of his bike and I thought: "Hey up, we might be in business here." And sure enough, I passed him on the last lap and bagged the 500 quid, and he ended up with next to nothing for limping home fourth or fifth. But that was a rarity. More often I'd be coming away with 50 or 60 quid from a day at Brands or wherever. More if I won both the 350 and 500 final, which happened quite a lot in the mid-Sixties, but it wasn't easy money.

At the 1965 Ulster Grand Prix John blew up both his 500cc Nortons and was quoted in *Motor Cycling*: "The last time I wrecked a Manx engine it cost £217 to repair. Since then spares have gone up and are harder to get. Some people think you can make a lot of money racing – they don't realise the expense."

Chris Carter: Let's talk about mechanics. Who did you have helping you?

Various people helped me over the years but they were really just assistants. I had a mechanic called Ernest Radford but everybody called him Bim. He used to help Norman Storer and then he came on board with me but he didn't do much more than drive the van to the meetings and push the bike on to the line and that was the same with most of my mechanics.

Alan Pike helped me later on. He was a painter and decorator and he would paint the numbers on my bikes before stick-on numbers came popular. I couldn't afford a proper paid mechanic. And looking back, no wonder Russ Warren made such a fuss of me. He bought the bikes through his employer, pocketed half the prize money, and I did all the preparation myself. I stripped my own engines and rebuilt them, changed the sprockets and tyres and I even did all the cleaning down when I got home.

A lot of silverware to polish! Trophy haul in 1964
(Cooper Collection)

Chris Carter: What about travelling to and from the meetings? I know from being a reporter back then the vehicles were slow, and without motorways the distances were longer and the journey times much greater.

From 1961 until 1965 when I opened my garage I worked with my dad at The Big Six, a clothing shop on Tennant Street in Derby. He wasn't the nicest man in the world, I can tell you, and when we closed the shop I used to go home and start working on my bikes, and I can remember on one occasion working until 3am on my Norton and then loading up and going straight to Snetterton, a difficult journey in those days, then sleeping for an hour or so in the back of the van before going out to morning practice.

Brands Hatch from Derby was a journey of about eight hours before the motorways – Loughborough, Leicester, Market Harborough, Rickmansworth, Denham, then straight through the centre of London. I can remember stopping at the Halfway House Cafe on the A5 on the way home one time and having a cup of tea with sidecar racer Owen Greenwood at two o'clock in the morning.

And I was going to Brands Hatch once and I came across Griff Jenkins broken down at the side of the road about 20 miles from the track. I had a towrope with me so I stopped and towed his van to Brands and when we got there I said: "You'd better not bloody beat me now!"

Right behind Griff Jenkins at Oulton Park in 1965
(Malcolm Carling Collection)

With Chris Conn in the paddock at the Dutch TT, 1966
(Unknown)

Chris Carter: What about travelling over to Ireland?

The first real road race I entered was the North West 200 in Northern Ireland. A bloke called Ollie MacChesnie ran it. I had to drive up to Liverpool, unload the bikes on to the boat, and then someone met me in Belfast with a car and trailer and took me up to Port Stewart.

One year several of us put our bikes on a train after the racing on Saturday, and once it set off for Belfast we were all frantically changing the sprockets on board and getting the bikes ready for a meeting at Cadwell Park the following day. In Belfast we caught the overnight ferry back to England, and first thing on Sunday morning we loaded the vans up at Liverpool and drove straight across to Cadwell, where they put on a special late practice for those of us who'd been competing in the North West.

We had to change the petrol tanks, the tyres, the sprockets and everything else on the train. You can't believe how things have changed. Nowadays a rider wouldn't dream of putting his bikes on a train, driving his own van, and getting his hands dirty. I did it all the time. Sometimes I had a helper, but not a paid mechanic, as such. Riders generally didn't then. There wasn't the money around.

WORKING WITH MY DAD

Chris Carter: You mentioned working with your father, and that it wasn't an entirely happy arrangement. Talk a little about that and why you did it.

For about four years in the early 1960s I worked for my dad at The Big Six gentlemen's clothing shop in Tennant Street in Derby, which I absolutely hated. It was the biggest mistake I ever made. In 1961 I was working as a mechanic for Minions but when my dad had an operation for ulcers and went into hospital I stepped in to help. It should have been a temporary thing and from the beginning I was always desperate to leave, but he had a hold over me. It was emotional blackmail really.

John posing with his father, Phil, at Kingsmead Service Station. Smiling here but their relationship was not always a happy one
(John Cooper Collection)

Working for my father handicapped my racing no end. My dad wasn't a nice man at all. He wouldn't give me time off, and he wouldn't even let me answer the phone, let alone use it to make calls, so it was hard to talk to circuit owners, trade people or the motorcycle press. He made life very difficult for me indeed. He wouldn't allow me to ride in the TT, and continental racing was completely out of the question, of course, so it was 1965 before I raced abroad.

I would regularly go home from work at six o'clock at night, then work on my bikes, finishing late at night, 10pm, 11pm or even midnight. And then my wife began suffering from a brain tumour, so I was leaving work at the shop, walking home, making tea and seeing if she was alright and only then could I prepare my bikes to go racing at places like Cadwell Park and Snetterton at the weekends.

There weren't many two-day meetings then, which is just as well because getting him to agree to let me go anywhere on a Saturday was nigh on impossible. I'd travel to the meetings early on a Sunday morning, or get there the night before and sleep in the van.

Generally speaking, practice would start at 8.30 in the morning, and then there'd be a 250cc, 350cc and 500cc heats and finals. I'd often ride in six races and three practice sessions all in the same day. Then the next day I'd be back at work at the shop.

Later on, in 1965, after I took the tenancy of Kingsmead Service Station, a brand new Cleveland garage on Ashbourne Road, my father came to work for me but the arrangement didn't last. My dad operated a driving school from my garage and he ran his car for virtually nothing. He was always filling it up without paying. I once worked out that based on the petrol he was actually buying, his Morris 1000 was doing about 600 to the gallon. On top of that he was selling petrol to his mates cheap, and it all came to a head one day when I was talking to a chap who had no idea who I was. He said: "If you ever want any oil or petrol there's a guy called Phil Cooper comes in the Traveller's Rest. His lad runs Kingsmead Service Station and he can get it for you cheap." That was the last straw and we agreed a parting of the ways.

Kingsmead Service Station opening day, 1965
(John Cooper Collection)

SIXTIES STORIES

Chris Carter: Tell us a few tales about racing in the 1960s.

Fine margins. A tricky moment at the TT, and being looked after by the marshals after a rare tumble at the Mallory Esses, which would later bear his name
(Mortons Archive)

Mike Hailwood was a really good sort, friendly and he spoke to everybody. One time Mike turned up somewhere without his wallet and he borrowed 20 quid off me, and for ages afterwards I kept saying: "Have you got that 20 quid you owe me?" "Oh yes," he'd say, "but I haven't got it on me." Then we were in a race together at Mallory Park. There was something wrong with his bike and I lapped him at the hairpin on the last lap on the way to winning the race. Afterwards he said: "You know that 20 quid I owe you? Well, we'll say it's square because I baulked those other lads who were right behind you, otherwise they might have passed you."

The way it was. Post-race analysis with Phil Read and Mike Hailwood
(Unknown)

I was very fortunate and in my racing career I never really found out motorbikes are dangerous, but I did have a few nasty injuries over the years. I once went to Aberdare Park in Wales and for some reason I felt particularly super-confident. Oh dear! I used to go really well at Aberdare Park. I held the lap record there for 13 years and beat Mike Hailwood and I could whiz around there like crazy.

So on this day I thought I'd make bad starts on purpose and have some fun passing everybody. The plan worked okay in the qualifying heat. I won it, and I thought I'd do it again in the final. Well, on the second or third lap Dave Degens fell off on the entrance to the paddock bend which was narrow with trees everywhere and his bike slid across the track. I hit it hard, flew over the bars, hit a tree and tore a big hole in my side you could put a fist into. I got up but felt a bit woozy and they took me, staggering, into the first aid tent.

The chap there smacked me on the chops a few times and said: "Whatever you do, don't pass out before the doctor gets here. Hold on to this pole in the middle of the tent and don't go unconscious whatever you do. Now is there anything you want me to get you?" I said I'd love a cup of tea. Off he went, leaving me clinging on to this pole, and while he was fetching the tea my mechanic, Bim, arrived, took one look at the hole in my side which was bleeding profusely and all but passed out. So when the steward came back he said: "I think he'd better have this cup of tea." So Bim had it and I had to wait for another one!

It was a nasty injury and when I got home I had to go to Derby Royal Infirmary every day for treatment and dressing changes. There was a terrifying matron

Giving Pat Nelson a lift, and chatting to Phil Read and Billie Nelson. Both pictures taken at the East German Grand Prix at the Sachsenring in July 1968

(Unknown)

there but I got friendly with a lovely nurse called Liz, who looked after me.

Yorkshireman Charlie Freeman was a sidecar racer. At the Isle of Man one year, Charlie tipped the sidecar up at the Gooseneck and both Charlie and his passenger Billie Nelson fell out. After they scrambled clear, Billie said to the marshal: "Tell Freeman he was going far too fast and he's a bloody idiot!" The marshal said: "Why don't you tell him yourself?" Billie said: "I can't, we've not been speaking for a fortnight."

I liked Billie Nelson a lot, and his wife Pat too. Billie was very superstitious. If he ever saw the moon through a window, he used to turn his money over in his pocket for good luck. He raced solos as well as sidecars and we travelled together to the Dutch TT one year. We planned to go on to the Belgian Grand Prix afterwards, but after the Dutch he said: "I'm sorry but I'm going to leave you now John, because I can't manage any longer without Pat." So I had to get someone else to take me and the bikes to Belgium while Billie went home and picked his wife up and joined us there later. It was touching they thought so much of each other.

Billie was killed in Yugoslavia, poor lad, racing a solo at the Yugoslavian Grand Prix. He was going round a bend and there were five-gallon drums marking the course and one was a little bit out. He cracked his knee on it and crashed.

One of my worst ever crashes was at the Ulster Grand Prix in 1966, practising on my 350 Norton. I was coming up to a fast right-hander called Bewdour at a hell of a speed and John Blanchard was up ahead, coasting in the middle of the road. I passed John on the outside but as I did so, he suddenly drifted across and shoved me into the grass bank. Whack! I hit the ruddy bank, went over the handlebars and tumbled a long, long way down the road, end over end. I was going at well over 100mph and it was really lucky I kept going in a straight line. Left or right and I'd have been killed. I once asked Dick Creith how fast to take Bewdour and he said: "As quick as you come to it sonny!"

Mike Hailwood saw it all happen and flashed past me while I was cartwheeling down the road. I got a lift back to the paddock on the back of a marshal's bike and when we arrived I was feeling very second-hand indeed. Mike was already there. "Bloody hell, John," he said. "I've never seen anything like it. I thought you were dead, at least!" I said: "I've felt better, Mike."

I was bruised black and blue all over and later on I stiffened up and started aching like hell. When I got back to my digs I ran myself a bath, but when I got in I slipped, fell backwards, cracked my head on the taps and knocked myself out. I was rooming with Brian Barlow, the chain fitter from Renolds, and he had to bring me round!

Speaking of John Blanchard, I can remember coming around Clearways once at Brands Hatch and going a bit wide. Down the ditch I went and back up the other side, losing a lot of ground, and while I was down there recovering the situation, John Blanchard came past. Later on, he wrote a letter to a team owner trying to get a ride, in which he said that his recent successes include beating John Cooper at Brands Hatch. But he didn't mention I was down in the ruddy ditch when he passed me!

Another accident from those times that sticks in my mind happened at Oulton Park. It was a bit damp on the first lap and I was well down in the pack because grid positions had been pulled out of a hat and I'd started last. Approaching the Shell Oils hairpin I could see Fred Stevens way ahead on a Paton flying up the hill from Knickerbrook, so I thought I'd better get a move on.

So I outbraked Joe Dunphy into the hairpin but I was going miles too fast and the bloody bike went sideways. Bang! I fetched Joe off, went up in the air, came down really hard and broke my collarbone. I smashed my glasses and nearly sliced my eyelid off too but the worst thing was I'd bent Joe's bike quite badly. I felt terrible.

The marshals laid me on the bank and Joe came walking past with his mangled bike. "Are you all right?" he said. "Not great," I said, "but I'm ever so sorry, Joe."

"Ah, don't worry about it," he said. But I felt so guilty that when I got home I posted him a blank cheque so he could get his bike repaired. I think he just took the minimum amount to get his frame straightened. Anyway, it made me feel a bit better.

When I went to Ray Pickrell's funeral a little while back, I heard Joe's wife Valerie say: "Who's that chap?" And Joe said: "That's John Cooper, the guy who knocked me off and then paid for my bike to be fixed."

I broke my collarbone at a meeting a couple of weeks before a big meeting at Mallory Park and after practice I asked Jack Walton, who was secretary of the meeting, if I could have a pusher off the back of the grid. He had no objections and gave me a ticket so I could do that, but

Big singles at Brands Hatch. John Cooper, 'King of Brands' Derek Minter and Joe Dunphy in 500cc action
(Nick Nicholls Collection, Mortons Archive)

Arthur Taylor, who was clerk of the course, found out and came to see me.

Arthur had a solicitor's bearing about him, and he wasn't a friendly man by any means. He was a stickler for procedure and the sort of man who would never say yes if he could say no. "Oh no," he said, "I can't allow that. You should have seen me earlier. You'll have to start off from your qualifying position on the front row and push the bike yourself."

So in the race I made a lousy start because of my bad shoulder, and when Bill Ivy fell off in front of me at the Devil's Elbow I hit his bike, went over the handlebars and re-broke my collarbone. The first person I saw when I picked myself up was Arthur Taylor. I was very angry and I let rip. After that I didn't speak to him for years until one day I was walking down Sadler Gate in Derby and he was coming the other way. I stopped him and said: "I think it's time we spoke, Arthur." We became friends again from then on. In fact, we became such good friends he left me some money in his will.

A funny story from the early Sixties involves a pal of mine, a rider called Monty Buxton from Ripley in Derbyshire.

Portrait of a road racer
(Nick Nicholls Collection, Mortons Archive)

I won the 500cc heat one weekend at Scarborough but when I was cleaning the bike down afterwards I found a crack in the frame. It didn't look too serious and I was going to go out in the final anyway but people persuaded me it was better to be safe than sorry.

Now Monty hadn't qualified for the 500 final and I wondered about borrowing his bike. It was sitting there in the paddock ready to go but even though I searched high and low, Monty was nowhere to be seen. Time was running out and in the end I decided he wouldn't mind, so I took the numbers off my bike, put them on his and off I went. Well, Monty was watching at the top of the hill with his wife, Sheila, and apparently he turned to her when the race started and said: "Do you know, that looks like my bike." Then on the next lap he said: "That looks ever so much like my bike," and on the third lap he said: "Bloody hell, that is my bike!"

I won the race and afterwards Monty came running up, quite pleased because I was his friend, but a bit cross at the same time because I'd used his bike without permission. In the end we split the prize money and it was smiles all round.

Mid Sixties

Leading the field into Druids Hairpin, Brands Hatch
(Mortons Archive)

Cresting the Mountain, Cadwell Park, September 1966
(Nick Nicholls Collection, Mortons Archive)

Good Friday, Brands Hatch, 1965. From left: Dan Shorey, Griff Jenkins, Derek Minter, Joe Dunphy, John Cooper and Paddy Driver
(Malcolm Carling Collection)

Sharing a joke with Derek Minter
(Mortons Archive)

Being chased by Paddy Driver, Silverstone, 1965
(Mortons Archive)

John Cooper, Derek Minter and Dan Shorey, on 350cc single-cylinder Manx Nortons, surround reigning double world champion Hailwood on his works Honda six. Oulton Park, March 1967
(Nick Nicholls Collection, Mortons Archive)

Leading the way. Devil's Elbow, Mallory Park
(Nick Nicholls Collection, Mortons Archive)

Brands Hatch, March 1967. John Cooper (350 Norton) leads Derek Minter, Dave Croxford and Ron Chandler
(Nick Nicholls Collection, Mortons Archive)

With the Evening News Trophy, Brands Hatch, August 1966
(Mortons Archive)

DOMIRACER

Chris Carter: You were on your Manx Nortons for most of the 1960s but you rode other bikes too.

I raced my Nortons for years but I rode all sorts of other bikes. One day I was at Snetterton with my 350 and 500 Nortons. I hadn't entered the unlimited race, but a chap came up to me and asked me to ride his Domiracer. I said: "Thanks but not really, I'm just packing up to go home." But he was very persuasive and I eventually caved in and went with him to see the organisers.

We got their blessing and even though I'd never seen the bike before I won the race. Back in the paddock, I was just leaning the bike up against this bloke's van when he came running up, so out of breath he could hardly talk. I said: "What's the problem?" He was red in the face. "We are splitting the money, aren't we?" he gasped. I think it was £100. I said: "I'll tell you what, as you were so keen on me riding it, I'll have two-thirds and you have a third."

He wanted me to carry on riding it after that. I said I was already committed but I introduced him to Geoff Barry, who rode it a couple of times. But then Geoff fell off and bent the frame. The chap rang me up and said: "You owe me a new frame." I said: "What's that got to do with me?" I ended up giving him a Manx frame and a pair of forks.

Curtis Domiracer, Snetterton, March 1968
(Nick Nicholls Collection, Mortons Archive)

Brands Hatch backwards on an evil-handling 650 BSA
(Unknown)

HUTCHINSON 100

Chris Carter: Wasn't there a time when you were paid danger money to ride a particularly evil-handling BSA?

Yes, I won the Hutchinson 100 production race in 1966 on a BSA 650 Spitfire which handled so badly the factory paid me danger money! The Hutchinson 100 meeting was run backwards at Brands Hatch and I loved it. My favourite part was going up Paddock Bend, which became an uphill left-hander. You could really get on the power and drive it up and over, which was a fantastic sensation.

What happened was in practice, along the bottom straight and round what had become a right-hander up to the hairpin, the bike was an absolute camel, wobbling and tank-slapping like crazy. Actually, it probably wasn't half as scary for me as it looked from the pits but it must have been a horrific sight, or let's say exciting

CHARLIE WILLIAMS

Grand Prix racer and eight times TT winner

I got interested in motorcycle racing from an early age and a significant reason for that was that, fortunately for me, I was born and grew up within earshot of Oulton Park race circuit. Initially, I was more interested in watching the car racing there, but that all changed when, aged around 13, I got hold of a beaten-up old Autobyk. I rode it round the garden again and again, and on subsequent visits to Oulton I began to see things somewhat differently.

It wasn't very long before I was completely hooked on motorcycle racing. In fact, I suddenly knew exactly what I wanted to do with my life and that was to become a professional motorcycle racer!

One rider in particular that I saw there influenced my decision and that man was John Cooper. As far as my mates and I were concerned around that time, you were either a Minter fan or a Cooper fan and I had both feet very firmly in the Cooper camp. John's flamboyant and exciting style was so different to that of all the other riders out there.

By the time I was 16 and old enough to ride on the road I had built myself a small Villiers-engined special with a fuel tank and seat borrowed from a 175 Bianchi. It had home-made rear-set footrests and clip-on handlebars. It wasn't actually very fast but it sure looked the part.

To complete the package I painted my pudding basin helmet red and stuck a pair of John Cooper Moon Eyes on the front. I would ride around the lanes on Cheshire, cornering with my knee out, trying for all I was worth to emulate my hero.

It would be three more long years before I would make it on to the racetrack myself, firstly as a sidecar passenger and shortly afterwards as a solo racer. And just two years later, during my first ever visit to Brands Hatch, I actually rode in the same race as John. It was to be the only time we shared the same race track but since then we have become good friends and I never tire of listening to John's wonderful stories about those magical racing days in the 1960s when I was one of his very many fans. No doubt many of John's fascinating stories are to be found throughout this book.

All hands to the pump. Refuelling the 650 BSA during a Thruxton 500 mile race. Team-mate Bill Ivy gets involved
(Unknown)

to say the least. Colin Shepherd was the BSA team manager and after practice he said: "Look John, if you don't want to ride it we'll understand, but if you do and you win the race we'll give you a £100 bonus."

I said I didn't mind giving it a go, so they gave me this what you might call danger money and I went out and won. Percy Tait's bike was faster than mine as well as better handling but I kept passing him going along the main straight and in the end I won the race. I couldn't understand it at all so afterwards I asked him what had been going on. He said the front brake adjuster on his bike had kept vibrating loose and he was having to tighten it up on the straight on every lap. That's how I managed to beat him.

Gunning it! 250cc Royal Enfield, Mallory Park, May 1964
(Nick Nicholls Collection, Mortons Archive)

Kentish machine in Kent. John at Brands Hatch on the 246cc Greeves
(Nick Nicholls Collection, Mortons Archive)

Heading Billie Nelson through Eau Rouge, Spa Francorchamps. Belgian Grand Prix, 1967
(Mortons Archive)

CONTINENTAL RACING

Jack chased by John: Findlay and Cooper at the East German Grand Prix, Sachsenring, 1968
(Jarda Sejk)

Chris Carter: It was obvious to me at the time you were good enough to race in grands prix, and sure enough, when you did break free from your dad and enter some grands prix you did very well indeed. Talk about your experiences on the continent, about the difficulties and costs involved, and why you didn't do more world championship races.

When I was free from my dad I started racing abroad. My first continental race was the Dutch TT at Assen in 1965. A chap called Henry Burik was the boss man there then and it was a job to get a ride even though I'd won a lot of races in England. A chap called Peter Chapman put a call in on my behalf and persuaded them to give me a start in the 350 and 500 grands prix and I did okay, finishing sixth and fourth respectively, then I fell off while leading the Belgian Grand Prix.

The following year I was fourth again in the 500cc Dutch TT and in 1967 I finished third in the Czechoslovakian Grand Prix. Agostini won it, Mike Hailwood was second, and I was third, beating the Swiss rider Gyula Marsovszky by a wheel. That was a bloody fast race I can tell you. And it was dangerous at Brno in those days – mountainous, and the road surface was not the best.

In 1968 I was third at the Dutch TT, fourth in the East German GP at Sachsenring behind Ago, Alberto Pagani and Jack Findlay; and sixth at the Belgian Grand Prix at Spa Francorchamps. I also had some good finishes at the TT and the Ulster Grand Prix which were world championship rounds at the time. Altogether not bad, and I'd have liked to have done more, but because of the economics of it and the need to keep on top of things at the garage back home, I could never commit to anything like a full season.

The European organisers would give you a little bit of start money, but not nearly enough to pay for the travelling costs. That's why I sometimes used to travel with Billie Nelson. It made it more affordable.

Another thing that made it difficult was not having a mechanic and having to do everything myself. In 1968 I fell off at the Sachsenring in practice and wore a hole in the front forks. I didn't speak much German but I could make myself understood and found out where I could get them mended. I found the place and sure enough they welded the forks up, line bored them inside and made a beautiful job of it. I got back to the circuit, put them back together again and managed to start the race.

And of course there was an acute shortage of competitive bikes in those days. We privateers were all riding Nortons that were made in 1960 or 1961. They were getting worn out, basically, and the magnetos weren't much good to start with.

Sometimes they would just stop, and I remember Reg Dearden saying at the TT one year the reason there was a wire attached to a Norton magneto was so that you could swing it round above your head and hurl it into the sea.

In the Sixties you'd got the Japanese factories with six or eight works riders between them on very fast bikes, riders such as Bill Ivy and Phil Read on Yamahas and Hailwood and Redman on Hondas. As a privateer you were at a serious disadvantage because the works bikes were doing 150mph down the straight whereas the Manx Nortons were doing 125.

Now don't get me wrong, Agostini was a very good rider indeed and tremendous at the TT. He won 15 world titles after all. But much of the time he was only riding against Manx Nortons and G50 Matchlesses.

In the last five or six years on MVs he had it pretty easy. He could leave everybody for dead.

Chris Carter: Was bureaucracy a problem? Thinking about the race organisers, officials, stewards etc.

There were jobsworths to deal with at the tracks and that eventually started to change in the late 1970s when Kenny Roberts came over. He said we're not putting up with this, standing in a queue for hours on end to get a piddling amount of start money. And then a certain Chris Carter and Mike Trimby and one or two others started getting changes made and MotoGP grew out of it.

But in the 1960s the riders weren't treated well and at the end of the decade I was asked by a journalist, maybe yourself, why I had stopped going to grands prix altogether. I said two good reasons were the money on offer was insulting, and I didn't appreciate having to queue for ages at the end of the day to collect a pittance.

I said at the time: "When I'm at work I don't treat my employees like rubbish, and they treat me like the boss. But as soon as I race motorcycles on the continent I'm treated like an idiot. Riders don't get any respect from the organising body. Invariably they are treated like animals. Organisers get the crowds too easily, and the crowd is cheated by a world championship tag. It's only a European championship... and not a very good one at that."

And I did feel a bit taken advantage of. I explained that only a couple of years previously I had been offered just £70 to ride in two classes at the Dutch TT, and that it was one of the better-paying circuits. I finished off by saying: "It seems to me that with attendances of 150,000 somebody is making a lot of money, and it isn't the riders."

The British ACU officials were not much help either. They were supposed to represent us but most of them were just over there on holiday and didn't know what was happening half of the time. Travelling was not without its difficulties either. In those days you had to have a carnet (international customs document), and when you got to Dover and Calais you had to wait in line at customs to have it stamped, and then again at every border you had to queue while everyone had their paperwork checked. It was a pain.

I can remember going to Aachen and standing there waiting to have the carnet stamped and a big Australian rider called Jack Ahearn went to the front of the queue and said: "I've been waiting long enough, I want my carnet stamped now," and the customs man said: "No, you wait." Well, a bit later the official left the room and Jack stamped his carnet himself, threw the counterfoil on his desk and said to us all: "Right, see you guys later. I'm off."

Another time, I went to Switzerland and the customs man wouldn't stamp the carnet because it was late at night. I said a few choice words about him but he spoke good English, which I hadn't realised, and he wasn't amused. So he locked the bloody office up and went home and I had to sleep in the van from 11 at night until nine in the morning when they opened up again.

Chris Carter: You mentioned Peter Chapman helped you get your first grand prix ride. I would guess a lot of people these days won't know who he was.

Peter Chapman ran a coach business in Northamptonshire. Peter used to have something to do with importing Kawasakis and he asked me if I'd go and do some test riding in Japan. I did get to do some testing at Fuji and I rode in the Japanese Grand Prix.

Chris Carter: Tell us about that.

The trip to Japan was a bit of a one-off. Sadly, the bikes weren't very competitive and they kept seizing up. In fact the trip was a bit of a disaster from start to finish really. When I got off the plane in Japan there was no one to meet me and nobody could speak any English. I wanted to go to the hotel but I couldn't make the taxi driver understand where I needed to go. But I eventually made myself understood to another taxi driver and later on some people from Kawasaki picked me up from the hotel and I went test riding for three days. Chris Vincent was there at the same time and Dave Simmonds was there testing a 125.

I was riding a twin-cylinder 500cc two-stroke, which was a fast machine while it was going but it just kept locking up, which was a bit frightening at 130 or 140 miles per hour down the straight. You had to be lightning quick with the clutch lever.

In good company.
Sharing a joke with Ago and Mike
(Mortons Archive)

Chris Carter: **I know you raced abroad quite often in non-championship meetings, particularly in Italy.**

I did quite a bit of non-championship racing in Europe from the mid-Sixties onwards. I first rode at Riccione in Italy in about 1966. John Hartle took a big group of us – Derek Minter, myself, Derek Woodman, quite a few others. From there we went to Rimini, Cesenatico,

350cc action from the 1965 Dutch TT. John Cooper leads Minter, Hartle and Driver. John finished sixth (Malcolm Carling Collection)

Milano Marittima, and on to Imola. It took us about five weeks altogether and it was a good way to start the season. Very enjoyable. But the circuits were dangerous. Tree-lined roads, twisting town streets, promenades along sea fronts. It was all stopped after Angelo Bergamonti was killed at Riccione in 1971.

I also raced regularly at the annual international meeting held at the Tilburg circuit in southern Holland. I won three classes in a day there in 1968 and I won there again in 1969 and 1971.

Montjuic Park near Barcelona was particularly twisty and turning, with buildings and trees everywhere. I raced there on an Ossa as team-mate to Santiago Herrero, the Spanish lad who got killed on the Isle of Man in 1970. Luigi Taveri had a rare outing on a 500cc MV when I was there and the straight was so bumpy, and he was so small and light, the big MV chucked him straight off!

The Ossa didn't turn out to be all that good, I'm afraid. In fact it seized up and I clattered into a tree. But it freed off and I managed to limp back to the pits.

I thought that was me done for the day

and I was quite relieved but to my horror they repaired it and I had to go back out.

The social side of racing abroad was great, going to bars and clubs afterwards with Mike Hailwood and co. We had a nice time and a lot of laughs. One night I said to Mike: 'Where's your car?' He said: 'I've just parked it on top of a heap of gravel.' He'd got it totally stuck and it had to be winched off the next morning with a crane.

Returning to the paddock late at night at the Belgian Grand Prix one year, Mike noticed Dan Shorey had parked his caravan on a hill so he let the handbrake off with Dan inside. It went rolling down the slope and banged into a bank.

Dan appeared at the doorway in his pyjamas and said: "I suppose you all think that's funny, do you?" Actually, it was rather amusing. And when I rode in Fuji, Peter Williams and Jack Findlay and I decided to go and have a sauna. There were these individual steam-heated sauna boxes, and this pretty girl would put you in this cabinet and close the lid so just your head was sticking out. Then she'd strip off and dance around in the nude. But I forgot to take my ruddy specs off and when she stripped off I couldn't see a ruddy thing because my glasses steamed right up! And there was no point calling out because she didn't speak any English.

No sign of pre-race nerves. Waiting on the start-line with countryman Phil Read
(Unknown)

Sharing the 500cc podium with Agostini and Hailwood, Czechoslovakian Grand Prix, 1967
(Unknown)

Continental Racing

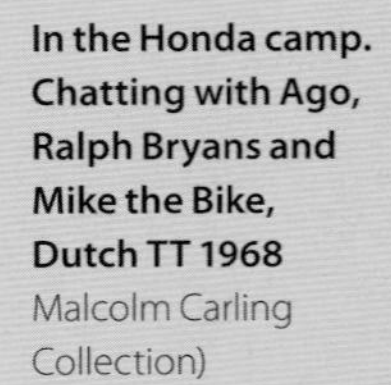

In the Honda camp. Chatting with Ago, Ralph Bryans and Mike the Bike, Dutch TT 1968
Malcolm Carling Collection)

Relaxing in the paddock at the Dutch TT
(Unknown)

Leading Italian ace Alberto Pagani
(Ronald Hunt)

On the pit wall at the Sachsenring with Rod Gould and Pat Nelson 1968
(Jarda Sejk)

Wheeling the Seeley on to the grid alongside Ago's works MV, East German Grand Prix, Sachsenring 1968
(Jarda Sejk)

1965 RACE OF THE YEAR

Chris Carter: You're particularly famous for beating Giacomo Agostini in the Race of the Year at Mallory Park in 1971, but you first won the event a long time before that.

I won the Race of the Year three times altogether and the first win was in 1965. I was fortunate because it started to rain a bit before the race, which made the track a bit damp and slippery, so Mike Hailwood on his works MV and Read and Ivy on their factory Yamahas couldn't use their bikes to their full potential. Checking the race reports from the time, I see I had no clutch for the last four laps but I didn't really need one at Mallory Park – I only ever really used three gears there on the Norton.

After the race, Mike Hailwood arranged for Chris Barber and his band to come and play at a function room at the circuit and we all enjoyed a bit of a party. When we were all well oiled they played the Sheik of Araby and they got me and Mike up on the stage. "I'm the Sheik of Araby, Your love belongs to me, At night when you're asleep, Into your bed I'll creep!" Bill Ivy got so drunk that night they pushed him into the back of his car and he curled up and went to sleep. Carol Stead, who was one of Mike's gang, drove him home.

Exiting Devil's Elbow at Mallory Park ahead of Percy Tait, Rodney Gould, John Blanchard and Ron Chandler (Mortons Archive)

LITTLE BILL

Chris Carter: Tell us about Bill.

Little Bill Ivy was a nice lad. He went from rags to riches and back to rags again. He was a good little rider, not tall, and no weight at all, and I believe Phil Read's biggest mistake was picking him to ride in the Yamaha team because Bill used to beat him. On a 125 Bill was the perfect size, smaller than Phil, and he was the first bloke to lap the TT course at more than 100mph on a 125. Incredible. And he used to beat Phil on a 250 occasionally too.

When Bill had a works Yamaha contract he bought himself a new Ferrari. He went to the TT and he said to Mike Hailwood: "Come on, I'll take you round the TT course." They'd only got as far as the Highlander and things were getting a bit hairy. Mike said: "Just take your time, Bill, you're gonna kill us both." But Bill didn't take any notice and they went round the left-hand bend at Greeba Castle, then the right, sliding it. They ran down the side of the wall, smashed the side of the car in and nigh on wrote the bloody thing off. It had to be sent back to Maranello to be repaired.

I once went to Snetterton on a practice day with Bill and sidecar racer Chris Vincent. A bloke from Lotus was there and he invited us to have a go in one of his cars. "Have a drive round and feel your way into it," he said. "Take it steady and see how you go." I had a nice, fast but steady drive round. So far so good. But then Bill Ivy got in, stuffed it straight into a bank and that was the end of that. The Lotus chap said: "Cheerio you lot, don't come back."

Bill went car racing full-time of course, but he ran out of money, was completely stony broke, and to pay for his four-wheel racing he had to come back to bikes. And of course he was killed on the Jawa.

John in the paddock with entrant Tom Kirby, and fellow riders Bill Ivy and Chris Conn (Mortons Archive)

BRITISH CHAMPIONSHIPS

Chris Carter: You were a multiple British champion in the 1960s but you haven't mentioned that.

I won a few British championships and for a while I made them a priority but later on there would often be a big international meeting on the same day as a points-scoring national championship round and I would give that priority, so it was all a bit odd really.

But for the record I was 350cc British Champion in 1964, 350cc and 500cc British Champion in 1966, and 250cc British Champion in 1968.

During the 1960s there was an incredible number of meetings in Britain. There was racing almost every weekend, often two meetings on consecutive days with a long drive between. In 1968 there were more than 30 national and international meetings in the British Isles.

1965 Race of the Year

Winning in the rain. Race of the Year, Mallory Park, 1965
(Ronald Hunt / Nick Nicholls Collection, Mortons Archive)

ROL
3
3

Chasing Bill Ivy out of the Mallory Park Hairpin in 1965
(Malcolm Carling Collection)

Governor's Bridge, Senior TT, 1964. John finished a highly creditable ninth on his debut, Pete Bettison (31) was 11th
Nick Nicholls Collection, Mortons Archive)

TT TALES

Chris Carter: Tell us about your memories of the TT. You were usually reasonably competitive in the Isle of Man, but I get the feeling the TT was never a huge priority for you. Is that an accurate assessment?

I'd have liked to have been a TT star, but I never had a lot of luck there. I was lying second in the Senior one year and the crankpin broke on the last lap at Sulby Bridge. That's as close as I got but I did have some respectable results. I first went across to the TT in 1956 when I was 18, just before I got called up for the army. I went for a week with the Minion family, because Peter Minion was riding a Gold Star in the Clubmans race. The first time I raced there myself was eight years later.

The TT was a world championship round and besides that it was quite the thing to do. People said: "Oh, you'll really enjoy it," and so I grew up wanting to race there and eventually I did, but it was always hard work. There was little money available, and you had to get there, do your own maintenance, it was tough.

For morning practice you had to get up at 4am, get washed and into your leathers, fetch the bike out of the hotel garage, ride it up to the start-line in the pitch black, maybe pouring down with rain, freezing cold, hardly able to see. And then you had to stand there shivering, waiting for the sun to come up and the mist to clear before setting off and doing a couple of laps. Then you'd maybe go back to bed for a couple of hours before getting up again and working to get the bikes ready for afternoon practice. It was hard work as a privateer on your own.

In those times people rented garages all over Douglas. You could walk round the back streets and everywhere you went you could see bikes being worked on, and you'd see them being ridden backwards and forwards to the paddock on public roads. But nowadays there are tents at the back of the paddock and it doesn't happen any more. Years ago you'd finish practice, have a cup of cocoa in the cocoa tent to try to warm up a bit then ride the bike through town and along the sea front, back into the garage. Not street legal, of course. It was fantastic really. Good fun.

I rode for Reg Dearden a couple of times. He had a motorcycle shop in Barlow Moor Road in Manchester and he had a lot of Nortons over the years, but his bikes were always off colour, never quite right, and he'd never got the spares. Oh, it could be an uphill struggle.

Reg Dearden's wife was related to the people who owned Norton so he got opportunities to buy race bikes from the factory from time to time, and some years he used to take about 12 bikes to the Isle of Man. People like Lew Ellis of Shell used to rent a bike for the fortnight for their signed riders and he usually had a few left over. I was riding for Reg one year and I was in his garage on the Island and a lad came in and said: "Lew Ellis has sent me down. He says you can fix me up with a 500, mine's packed up." "Yes," said Reg, "that's no problem. I've got one available and I'll get John here to prepare it for you. Come down later on and it'll be ready."

And when the guy had gone he said to me: "Right John, clean that bike up a bit, gear it down a cog, and screw the throttle down so there's only three-quarter movement." Later on the lad came back and Reg said: "Right, here's the bike. If you can lap at 97mph on it tomorrow I'll put the special hammer cam in it for you." So off the lad went and the next day he went round at 96 and a half and Reg said: "That's close enough, you've nearly made it. Drop the bike off and come back in two hours."

Then, while he was away, I unrestricted the throttle and geared it back up, and after the next practice session the chap came back and said: "Bloody hell, Reg, that cam is something else, I can't tell you the difference it's made." And off he went happy as Larry.

Reg was a character. He used to take his wife's jewellery to the Isle of Man and take young birds out and lend them a gold bracelet or a diamond brooch or a nice ring for the evening. On the boat going across one time I was with Reg and we got chatting to a girl with a very short skirt on and her friend. "Come and have a drink with me tonight in the Castle Mona Hotel," he said, and generally made himself out to be a bit of a big shot. Sure enough they turned up and he lent her a very expensive brooch to wear for the evening. After a bit she went off to the toilet and he never saw her or the brooch again.

He once took a Jaguar E-Type to the Island, as he always liked to have a good car to take girls out in. He put the brakes on sharpish for some reason and the Norton spares he had in the boot slipped forward and tripped an engine cut-out switch that Reg didn't know was there. The engine stopped and it wouldn't start again. He asked me to help and I couldn't get it going either but then I said: "Let's start from basics, what exactly happened?" I looked in the boot, lifted the spares up and there was this bloody switch!

With Manchester wheeler-dealer Reg Dearden in 1965
(Nick Nicholls Collection, Mortons Archive)

Back at his premises in Manchester, Reg Dearden had tons of spares. I'll give you an idea. Before the war, someone turned up at his place with a van-load of footrest rubbers, gear lever rubbers, handlebar rubbers etc., and he said to Reg: "Do you want to buy any?" Reg said: "How much for the lot?" He bought them all there and then, including the van.

He was selling those rubbers right through into the 1960s. The rubbers worked out at a penny apiece and by the end he was selling them for half a crown or three bob. He had literally tons of spares.

He once booby-trapped a cupboard full of his best spares with bungee rubbers to keep people out but unfortunately it was his son Nigel who opened the cabinet and – whack! He got smacked in the face by these straps. It blacked his eye and his face was a mass of bruises for weeks.

I once went out for the night in Douglas with Reg. We were in a taxi and Reg said to the driver: "I'm looking for a chap called

On a rocking horse in the TT paddock, 1965
(Mortons Archive)

250cc Lightweight TT, 1965. Going well on the Greeves, and parked up at Braddan Bridge
(Nick Nicholls Collection, Mortons Archive)

Reg Dearden, he owes me some money. If you can tell me where to find him, I'll pay you well for the information." And the taxi driver said: "Reg Dearden is a good bloke. He's been coming here for years and he brings loads of bikes. He's a good man as far as I'm concerned so even if I knew where he was I wouldn't tell you." When we got out of the cab Reg said to the driver: "Here's a two quid tip, my name's Dearden." A generous tip in those days.

One year when I was riding for Reg Dearden at the TT, a company called Brearley-Smith made me an all-in-one seat and petrol tank unit for my Norton. It was a strange-looking thing that was perhaps a little ahead of its time. After practice Reg said: "Someone's just been in and told me they saw you going down Bray Hill on a rocking horse!"

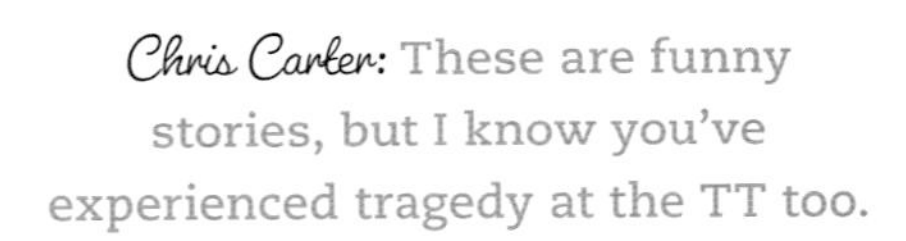
Chris Carter: These are funny stories, but I know you've experienced tragedy at the TT too.

Toshio Fuji got killed in the Isle of Man in 1966 when I was sharing a room with him. That was hard to deal with. He was such a nice lad, and we used to travel around together a bit. When he first came over to Europe he couldn't speak any English, but within a week he was managing really well. I lent him a 500 Norton to ride in the Belgian Grand Prix and he converted the gear-change and the back brake to the opposite sides, like on Japanese bikes.

It was the year of the ferry strike and the TT was run a few months later than normal. He was on a works 125cc Kawasaki and he kept having technical problems with the bike. Eventually some parts came over from Japan and the ACU told him he had one more chance to lap at a certain qualifying speed otherwise he wouldn't be allowed to race. He went out to give it a good go but at May Hill he drifted wide, hit the wall and killed himself. Actually, he got up and walked away but he'd punctured his spleen and he died later in the cottage hospital nearby. If he'd been taken to Nobles Hospital in Douglas he'd probably have survived.

After I found out he'd died I went back into our shared room and it upset me quite a bit seeing all his stuff lying there just as he'd left it. I thought: "Bloody hell, I'm off home."

John Cooper at speed on the 500 Seeley, 1970 Senior TT
(Nick Nicholls Collection, Mortons Archive)

250cc Lightweight TT, 1967 on a Kawasaki two-stroke. After the bike seized, John pushed in to finish 25th

Chris Carter: And what about your racing experiences over there? You say you never had much luck.

I definitely didn't have a lot of luck at the TT. In 1965, the year before Toshio died, I rode a factory 250 Greeves in the Lightweight race. I rode it at a couple of short circuit meetings and Bert Greeves asked me if I'd do the TT on it. It was nothing really special, and not really up to the standard of the Italian Mondials and Aermacchis that were out there, but I was going okay and hurtling down to Braddan Bridge when the flywheel came whizzing off the end of the crankshaft and overtook me!

My best TT result was fourth. But in 1971 I was running second to Agostini on a Seeley and although the engine had been rebuilt by Colin Seeley himself, the new crankpin he'd bought for the job hadn't been chamfered and on the last lap with less than 20 miles to go, the bloody thing broke at Sulby Bridge so I didn't finish. If he'd left the engine alone and not rebuilt it, it'd have probably been all right, but he tried to make sure it was perfect.

Another year I was on a Kawasaki two-stroke and holding fifth on the last lap when it stopped dead and I had to push in from Brandywell. The bike belonged to two RAF lads who were stationed in Singapore. It was really quick and in the race I was passing people left, right and centre. The lads were signalling at the Gooseneck and I got there well before they were expecting me, so much so they missed me completely on the first two laps. They thought I'd broken down so they packed up and went back to Douglas!

I might even have won that race but for a dimwitted marshal. The two-stroke oil tank was under the seat and you had to lift the filler cap a sixteenth of an inch to vent it. When I went into the pits to refuel and top up the oil, a marshal saw this cap wasn't fully closed and pushed it down. That cut the air off and with about a quarter of a lap to go the bike seized up for lack of oil. In 1970 I raced a Honda CB750 in the Production TT and finished ninth. Alf Briggs got it for me which was very good of him, but he was so careful with Honda's money he wouldn't sanction releasing a large petrol tank from the stores. Using a standard tank I had to stop far more often and it cost me a great deal of time over the five laps of the race.

Something completely different. Hustling a Honda four through Union Mills in the 1970 750cc Production TT
(Nick Nicholls Collection, Mortons Archive)

Pushing off alongside Chris Conn at the start of the 1967 Senior TT
(Mortons Archive)

John's 500cc Manx Norton's rear wheel floats at speed at the bottom of Bray Hill
(Nick Nicholls Collection, Mortons Archive)

At Quarter Bridge, Senior TT, 1967
(Nick Nicholls Collection, Mortons Archive)

On the Ray Petty Manx Norton, Signpost Corner, 1967. John finished fourth
(Nick Nicholls Collection, Mortons Archive)

Through Parliament Square, Ramsey on the way to eighth in the 250cc Lightweight TT. John's Padgett Yamaha was a little outgunned
(Nick Nicholls Collection, Mortons Archive)

Chris Carter: Like me, you've always got on well with the sidecar fraternity in the paddock. I think it's fair to say they're something of a breed apart. Tell us about some of the sidecar racers you've known, and I know you've raced as a passenger once or twice.

Sidecar drivers are definitely a breed unto themselves and I like them a lot. They're old-fashioned and friendly and they help each other out. These days the works riders and even the mechanics aren't allowed to mix with one another. Not like my day when we'd sit on the back of someone's van and have a cup of tea and a good chat. We'd lend each other parts, or even a complete bike.

Bill Boddice was a friendly chap I got on well with and I had a good friendship with Chris Vincent. I rode in the sidecar with Chris at the West German Grand Prix, and also at Mallory Park. I was at the Nurburgring on my solo and Chris's regular passenger didn't turn up. The ACU official there agreed that it'd be okay for me to step in, so that's what happened. I did a couple of practice sessions and then went out with him in the race, but it was so freezing cold it started to snow, and after a while my hands were numb and I could hardly hold on. I was knocking him on the knee to get him to stop but he ignored me and after the race I mentioned it. "Oh," he said, "I thought you meant go faster."

Passengering for British sidecar ace Chris Vincent
(Nick Nicholls Collection, Mortons Archive)

It's not as easy as it looks, being a passenger. There's more to it than leaning over the back wheel on rights and hanging out of the sidecar on lefts. You have to time your moves or it isn't possible to get across. But when I rode with Chris at Mallory Park he said: "Don't worry too much about moving around. All you have to do is sit there. A bag of spuds would be good enough for me. I don't really

STUART HICKEN

Superbike race team owner, leaseholder of Mallory Park circuit

John Cooper was a terrific rider, unbelievable. I was a huge racing fan in the 1960s and I was a dedicated Cooper helmet man so I probably knew more about John than he knew about himself. He was my hero and an inspiration to me when I raced a bit myself in the 1970s and early 80s and it's been an absolute privilege to become his friend in more recent years.

In the 1960s the domestic scene was super-competitive. It was a fabulous era with very big crowds and more so than nowadays the riders each had their own recognisable style of crash helmet. You could stand at Mallory Hairpin and see them coming into the Esses and reel them off... Cooper, Croxford, Chandler, Williams, Shorey, or whatever, and see exactly what was going on from the crash helmets alone. It was important too because every week any one of 20 guys could win a race.

In the 1960s there was a thriving motorcycle club in my home town of Coalville, with around 80 lads actively following British racing. Everybody had their own favourite rider. One guy would have a Chris Conn crash helmet, another a Joe Dunphy one. We all had a crack and I was lucky to be a Cooper man because I had more opportunities to rule the roost and take the Mickey than most of them.

The thing that appealed to me about John was his riding style was so completely different. He was the first man to hang off a motorcycle. He was spectacular and way ahead of his time. If the bike handled, he was going to do the business on it for sure. He was the man you'd want on your motorcycle.

John was quick at tracks all over the country but because there was no Donington Park then and Mallory Park was his local circuit, he had a huge following there and for sure he would always rise to the occasion there and ride out of his skin. He was an absolute master at Gerards and the Elbow and of course the Esses were named after him. There are not many people who have had that sort of accolade.

He was quick on the roads too, winning races in Ireland and on the continent, and although a TT win eluded him he got up to third place there in 1967 on a 250 Kawasaki before it seized up and broke down. He was pushing the bike in and it was ridiculously hot, and as he came out of Governor's Dip where I was standing, watching, he got his helmet off to cool down a bit and a policeman stopped him on the footpath and gave him a sweet. Many years later I surprised him by reminding him of it and he said: "How the bloody hell did you know that?"

The Yamsel which John invented proved to be a significant motorcycle, not least for Colin Seeley. It kept the name Seeley right at the forefront of British racing. No longer was there just the G50 Matchless Seeley but something with a very different engine. I think Colin Seeley got quite a few commissions because of John doing the business on the Yamsel as well as selling quite a number of Yamsel frame kits. John was unbelievably brilliant on it.

He won the Race of the Year on it in

need a passenger on a kneeler outfit." He actually wrote that in a column in one of the bike papers, which no doubt upset a few passengers.

But Chris was an exceptionally good driver in his day and he knew exactly what he could do with the passenger barely moving. I can't say I enjoyed either experience. I don't fully understand how passengers could do it so enthusiastically. I've known a lot of them over the years and I said to a girl passenger at a club meeting recently: "Bloomin' 'eck, you must be brave." She'd just won her race and she clearly loved what she was doing. In fact the enthusiasm at club meetings in general is great to see. They race for fun of course, there's no money in it, and they enjoy it a great deal.

Some of the people doing it are in their sixties, and a few of them were riding when I was. I'm over 80 now and they're still having a go. Incredible!

I always got on well with the continental sidecar lads, the Germans Max Deubel and Georg Auerbacher; and the Swiss drivers Fritz Scheidegger and the crazy Florian Camathias, who rode his racing outfit from Dover up to Liverpool to go across to the TT.

Totally illegal, of course. Camathias was a nice bloke and a good driver but his bikes weren't prepared as well as they might be. Some welding broke and that's why he lost control and was killed at Clearways at Brands Hatch.

I was particularly friendly with Max Deubel and I used to stop at his house in Beilstein, West Germany. And in 1965 when I won the Race of the Year at Mallory Park and won a thousand guineas, I gave the then world champion Fritz Scheidegger £100 to get me an 18ct gold Omega watch. He brought it over the following year and then in 1967 he brought me an 18ct strap to go with it. Sadly, he crashed at that very meeting and was killed.

After he retired I got to know Eric Oliver, who was a four-time world sidecar champion in the 1940s and 1950s, and I'm still in touch with Eric's son, who used to work at Rolls-Royce in Derby.

He raced a bit and I got him a Yamaha from America. I was also friendly with Owen Greenwood, who made the weird and wonderful Mini special which made him quite unpopular with the other sidecar drivers. He found ways round all the rules and regulations, a bit like Rolf Biland 10 or 20 years later. Both were clever and inventive people, like a lot of sidecar men.

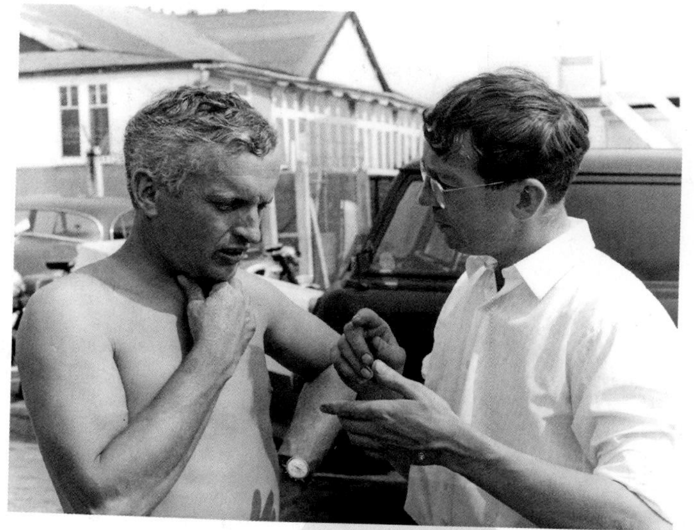

Talking to German star Georg Auerbacher (sidecar TT winner and three-time world championship runner-up) at Brands Hatch in August 1969
(Nick Nicholls Collection, Mortons Archive)

Messing about in the TT paddock, 1970
(Nick Nicholls Collection, Mortons Archive)

1970 and he wouldn't know that during the practice session held on the preceding Saturday afternoon I was standing on the inside of the Elbow by the marshals' post. As he came out of the hairpin I saw something running out of the bike underneath. I was jumping up and down and waving like a madman but he didn't see me and of course when he arrived at the Elbow he went straight down on his backside. The gearbox drain plug had come out. Evidently they repaired the bike and he won on it the next day.

It's a privilege now to have John as a friend. People I like and admire, like Sir Alex Ferguson and Brian Clough, have always been characters who, if they don't like or agree with you, just bloody well say so. Life's often easier that way, and I'm sure my wife would say I'm exactly the same. I don't suffer fools around me so I think I like that sort of character.

Sure enough, John is very truthful, very direct and straightforward. If he's your friend, he's a good person to have on your side. And although he might not come over that way to most people, he's also sensitive and generous. He's a very kind-hearted guy and sometimes he'll tell me he's helped someone out by lending them money and I'll think wow, that's a brave move, rather you than me.

John gets nowhere near the credit he deserves for his achievements. I don't know if it was the fact he was so to the point and such a blunt person that stopped him getting a works ride but he definitely deserved one. Like a lot of other riders, John would ride in two or three classes in a day. These days most riders will claim to be specialists on one type of bike or another, whereas then the best guys just jumped on any type of bike and rode it. I can tell that John can see himself in Bradley Ray, a tall, thin bespectacled young lad in my Superbike team who rides a bike differently to other people around him. John is very keen to see Bradley do well and I like that. It's nice too that whereas many ex-riders often say to younger ones, listen lad, you should be doing this or that, you don't ever hear John saying that. He appreciates we're in a totally different era and motorcycles are ridden very differently now. In fact, he has said to me he doesn't think he could have ridden a modern Superbike.

But actually, I don't agree with him there. Because John had a pure and natural talent like Mike Hailwood, and like George Best and Paul Gascoigne in the football world, if he'd been born later he'd still have been a top rider. A natural, instinctive ability like John's can't be taught. Fast then, fast now.

I know John regrets a little bit that he didn't get a factory ride and become a grand prix regular but nonetheless people all over the world know John Cooper. Just this year I was talking to some Yoshimura people at the Suzuki factory out in Japan and John's name came up. Ah, they said, the man with the Moon Eyes! John and his crash helmet are known throughout the motorcycling world.

NORTON LONGEVITY

Chris Carter: Your Nortons gave you great service for many years, and you and many other riders used them for many thousands of racing miles. They were quite remarkable in this regard, especially when you consider that today a new bike is not expected to be competitive for more than a couple of seasons.

Manx Nortons went on and on. The last ones were produced at Bracebridge Street in about 1960 or 61 and I was still riding them in 1967 until I switched to riding Colin Seeley's G50 Matchless.

There were occasional blow-ups but generally speaking they were reliable. You didn't have to do too much to keep a Norton going. We'd take them to bits and put them together every now and again, but usually only to do the usual straightforward stuff. A Manx Norton would do about 250 miles without there being any need to take the head off, and a big end would last two or three seasons. We never had to take the crankshaft apart.

I used to struggle with cracked pistons and it wasn't until I got a bit older and wiser that I found out I should have had the bike re-sleeved because the bore was worn and the pistons were slapping and getting cracked. Nobody ever told me, of course, and I had to learn the hard way.

Scotsman Joe Ryan had the so-called Fireplace Nortons. Goodness me, they were dirty, scruffy bikes but they were fast. I think he had a short-stroke Norton before anybody else. He rang me up one day shortly before the North West and he said: "Can you bring a pair of swinging arm legs across for me?" I said: "Yes, certainly Joe, pleased to help." So I took the legs across to Ireland and he gave them to Dick Creith, who was riding one of his Nortons. Ian McGregor was riding the other and he immediately said: "Hey, what about my bike?" "Oh very well," said Joe, have one each then!" So they both had one new 'un and one old 'un.

Joe's Nortons were always incredibly scruffy. He used to put cement dust in the rims rather than clean the oil out of them, and when I borrowed one of his bikes once and tried to clean the rims out he said: "Dinnae make them glatter sonny." He didn't want his bikes glittery.

Chris Carter: Was there any cheating? Were there oversized engines out there?

Sometimes I wondered if some people didn't have a 'special' of some sort. Occasionally Derek Minter would pass me down the straight and I'd think, "Well..." But then again he was only a little chap and he was a very good rider.

You could put a fee down and demand a test. At the TT they always strip and examine engines and I can remember one poor bloke had rebored his bike and taken it fractionally over the 500cc limit. It was only over by a minuscule amount but they disqualified him. I felt really sorry for him, he hadn't been cheating in the slightest.

MIKE'S HONDA

Chris Carter: You rode Mike Hailwood's 500cc Honda once or twice, I recall.

After Mike Hailwood stopped racing for Honda full-time he got to keep a 500/4 that had a frame made by Ken Sprayson of Reynolds. In 1969 I was chatting to Mike one day and I said: "Is there any chance of borrowing that four-cylinder Honda of yours? I wouldn't mind having a ride on it in the bank holiday meetings coming up at Snetterton and Oulton Park."

Being the nice guy he was he said: "Yes, you can borrow it if you want but beware, it's very difficult to steer. When you fall off at Snetterton you'll be sure to leave some marks on the road. I'll be looking out for them when I'm car racing there on the Monday!"

Well, he wasn't wrong. It was unbelievably bad to ride and hard to steer, wobbling and weaving and shaking its head all the time. My wrists swelled up so much from wrestling the thing I couldn't zip the cuffs up on my leathers. But oh boy, was it fast. On the long straight at Snetterton parallel with the A11 it was just incredible. Percy Tait was on a Triumph and the Honda was 25mph faster. I could pull 100 yards on him there but through the corners it was such a handful he'd catch me up again. Nonetheless I held him off and I was leading the race with about two laps to go when it started to rain. I opened it up coming on to the start-finish straight and the bloody thing went over on its side and I scraped the numbers off the fairing. Somehow I hung on and it flipped itself back upright and I carried on. Bill Boddice said later: "Ooh, that was lucky!"

A few came past while I was sorting myself out and I finished fourth in the end but I won my heat on it earlier on. It was an awful bike to ride and it was a good job really that at Oulton Park the following day a coupling broke in practice so I couldn't race it again. I don't know how Mike did so well on it. Joe Ryan said: "You couldnae keep it in a 10-acre field.'

John Cooper on his faithful 500cc Norton, leading John Blanchard on the ex-Minter Seeley prototype that John would take over and go on to own for more than 50 years
(Mortons Archive)

Jumping aboard at Snetterton while Peter Williams powers away on the Arter Matchless
(Nick Nicholls Collection, Mortons Archive)

A push from Mike's mechanic Nobby Clark
(Nick Nicholls Collection, Mortons Archive)

Leading across the line
(Mortons Archive)

Two days later at Oulton Park, practising with Malcolm Uphill and Stan Woods
(Mortons Archive)

The Honda squats under power
(Mortons Archive)

Hounding Phil Read and Mike Hailwood (Seeley), world champions both
(Unknown)

WORKS TEAMS

Chris Carter: I know you feel a little bit disappointed to this day that you didn't get to do a full season of grand prix racing on a more competitive bike. Why do you think you were never offered a factory ride?

Even though I won four British championships in the Sixties I was never offered a ride on a works bike. That was a shame because when I did ride on the continent I did quite well. I think I was ever so capable of winning some grands prix and even a world championship and I don't feel I really got the opportunity to show my ability. I often wonder what might have been.

Working for my dad definitely held me back quite a bit but apart from that, perhaps it was something to do with my attitude or my personality. Perhaps the team managers just didn't like me. Or maybe it was because people thought I could win on short circuits but grand prix tracks would be a different story. Who knows? I certainly didn't ever creep round the people who were running the teams, and the riders who already had works contracts had a lot of say.

Now Ralph Bryans was a nice chap and I liked him a lot, and he was a good little rider. So was Tommy Robb. But I never thought Ralph was better than me and I thought the same about Tommy. These people did as well as they did because they had very fast works bikes and because they were so small and light. When Honda had their little grand prix 50s and 125s these guys who were only 5ft 6in and seven or eight stone were ideal for them.

On the Seeley Matchless, dicing with Phil Read on his exotic works Yamaha four, Cadwell Park 1968
(Nick Nicholls Collection, Mortons Archive)

Chris Carter: I can tell you it wasn't all wine and roses being a works rider. Hugh Anderson once told me he hated the Suzuki factory. Not because the employees weren't pleasant people in many ways, but because of the works team's lack of consideration and empathy for the riders.

Suzuki riders used to crash in testing a lot because the bikes were seizing up all the time and Hugh would be spat off at a high-speed part of the track, down and hurt. There'd be no first aid people there, not even any marshals, and he'd be left lying alone on the ground waiting for the mechanics to turn up in their little van. And when they got there, the first question they always asked him, no matter how injured he was, was never, "How are you?" It was always "What did the bike do?" or "How's the bike?".

And that was because the bike was a special piece of equipment, difficult to build or put back together, whereas there was a queue of riders waiting to take Hugh's place.

At close quarters with Mike Hailwood, Silverstone, 1965
(Ronald Hunt)

MONEY

Chris Carter: Let's talk about money. While you were racing you always had a job or ran a business. Why was that?

A lot of riders in the 1960s and 70s only did motorbike racing. Like footballers who just played football, they never thought about the future. Footballers today earn so much money they don't have to worry, but that was not always the case. But all through my career in motorbike racing I always worked or had a business.

Thinking about packing up racing and having nothing else to take its place and provide an income always scared me. I was born in 1938, and during and after the war, life was hard for our family. We had no money to buy anything, and we were far from alone in this. We couldn't afford meat, we couldn't buy clothes, we needed coupons for our shoes, coupons to buy an ounce of sweets, and sixpence was a lot of money. And after the war most things were still on ration and I can remember my dad saying we can only get one bag of coal this week, we can't afford two.

Life was a struggle and it has made me very careful with money ever since. You never really get over it and I've never wasted money for the sake of it. I've never blown it on cars and suchlike. Now, as a result of being careful, I'm comfortable, and that's how I always wanted it.

But when I first got a motorbike I could barely afford to put petrol in it, and even into the 1960s I was having to budget very carefully all the time. Fortunately I was always able to win some money to maintain my bikes and get to the next meeting.

Later on I earned some good money from racing but I was not always paid what I was worth. There were many times I had very poor start money compared to

Not a man known for sitting on the fence. John Cooper at Snetterton
(Mortons Archive)

Racing in blinding hail, March 1967. Pat Mahoney takes a moment to wipe his goggles
(Mortons Archive)

some of the people I was racing against. Unless you stick up for yourself, people don't give you what you're worth, they give you what they can get away with. In general they were always tight with me because I was always a bit soft natured and never much good at negotiating.

I would have liked the opportunity to have a works ride, but it never came my way. I sincerely believe if I'd had a factory bike I could have won a world championship in the 1960s, but I often think to myself that in the end I was fortunate not to have a works contract after all. I was at my garage one Friday night, Kingsmead Service Station on Ashbourne Road, just below where a certain Chris Carter used to live, and a bloke came in and told me he'd just got the sack from BestKnit, the knitting factory about 50 yards away. "It'd make you a nice garage for you," he said. That set me thinking. I went along to have a look and the chap was right. Eventually I got a loan and bought it for £12,500. It was about 7000 square feet.

Now if I'd been away at all the grands prix with Mike Hailwood, Bill Ivy, Frank Perris and all that lot, hoteling it, living the high life, buying Ferraris and goodness knows what else, I'd have never have got that tip-off and bought those premises at Chandos Pole Street. I ran it as a garage for many years and in time I bought the land at the side of it and built two industrial units. I rent it all out now and get a bit of a pension off it.

If I'd been offered a works contract, flying all over the world staying in hotels blowing my money, I probably wouldn't have got any of that. So in many respects I was lucky. Okay, I never got to find out how I would have got on for a works team at the very highest level, but you can never have the best of both worlds. Things work out one way or another and you just have to go along with it.

On balance I was pleased not to have joined the jet-set brigade. Normally on a Sunday night while they were partying I'd be on my way home, ready to start work the next day. But the factory riders didn't work or have successful businesses and they weren't well off in the long run.

Mike Hailwood was without a doubt the best rider in the world, and he was a damned decent bloke, a very decent man indeed. He was always very chatty and gregarious, and he went to parties and socialised a lot, and it's a shame he ended up with no money. I don't know quite what happened and of course it's none of my business. His dad was said to be a millionaire and he certainly always seemed to be very wealthy, and Mike always looked to be very well off too. Then all of a sudden Mike had nothing.

He was an international playboy I suppose, which is an expensive lifestyle to maintain, and if you don't earn anything your money eventually runs out. I don't think Mike was particularly keen on work, or careful with his cash.

When Bill Ivy got his works Yamaha ride, the first thing he did was buy a brand new Ferrari and smash it up in the Isle of Man. Then he bought a flat above Mike Hailwood's pad in Heston, leading the high life, and left motorcycling behind to race cars. But he soon ran out of money, went back to motorcycle racing, fell off and killed himself. Tragic, really. Like Mike and some of the others, he only lived for today.

In about 1961 Jim Redman told me he had received an astonishing £15,000 from Honda. That was a colossal sum in those days. I never wanted to end up with no money so I always carried on working.

I've worked very hard and in retirement it's paid off. I'm not rich but I'm comfortable. I've some rental income which gives me a nice little pension so it's worked out very well.

Phil and Mike get into a tangle at the Ulster Grand Prix
(Unknown)

Neck and neck with Bill Ivy
(Mortons Archive)

TRADE SUPPORT

Chris Carter: You may not have had much sponsorship in your career, but what about support from the trade?

At the grands prix and other continental meetings, the top works riders were getting good start money but the rest of us were surviving on scraps. I got £200 start money in Italy once and I'd earn a few bob in prize money, but it was costing me around £100 a time to get out there. And the organisers treated the riders really badly. More than once we all had to queue in the rain to get paid out.

The ACU was more of a hindrance than a help. It was run by old-fashioned stick-in-the-muds who wouldn't agitate for change. They wouldn't even let you put any adverts on your bike until 1971. If somebody gave you a few quid to help you that couldn't be advertised on the bike. Ridiculous. A modest Castrol or Ferodo logo was allowed, but anything non-trade wasn't permitted. All you could put on the fairing were great big race numbers.

Trade support was better then though, and if you were winning regularly in the UK you could get away without having to buy too much in the way of consumables. Shell, Castrol, Renold, Dunlop and the like would give the top riders free oil, chains, tyres or whatever, which was a big help. I'd appear in magazine adverts when I won or got placed in a big race but I wasn't paid for that, and later a large ad featuring me with the caption, 'John Cooper reads Motor Cycle News' would appear regularly in a certain publication. I didn't get paid for that either. But Castrol and Shell and people had bonus schemes whereby they'd give their riders a few quid if they won and I did okay out of that.

And sometimes I got a decent bonus at the beginning of the year, which was handy. I had a contract with Duckhams towards the end of my career and I appeared in their colour ads. They agreed to pay me so much for each win but as the season went on they realised it was costing them a lot more than they thought. They became a bit reluctant to keep paying me and I don't think I got all of it in the end!

TYRES

Chris Carter: What about tyres? I know you had a close relationship with Dunlop.

I used to do a lot of testing for Dunlop. I tested their triangular tyres with Bob McIntyre and Alan Shepherd, and in the mid-Sixties at Oulton Park I tested the first set of slicks Dunlop ever made. Tony Mills was the boss then and when they first put slicks on my 500 Norton I was very wary of them to say the least, but he said: "Don't look at the tyres, John. Just ride it and tell us what you think." I didn't know what on earth to expect. Avons were considered the tyres to have then, and because Dunlop's tyres were triangular, a lot of people including Derek Minter didn't like them because of the way they made the bike fall into the corners. But I got used to them and grew to really like the way they behaved. I loved these triangular Dunlops but very few people used them.

I remember once going to Mallory Park to do some testing with Tony Mills and the Dunlop boys. John Hartle was there with some supposedly supersonic Avon tyres, the absolute bee's knees apparently. But after I passed Hartle coming out of Gerards and cleared off into the distance, he pulled in and Avon loaded up their truck and went home. And later when Avon packed up racing and a lot of riders had to switch to Dunlops, I was riding rings around people for quite a while until they got used to them.

Another time at Mallory Park I had just got some new Dunlop tyres fitted, and I was chatting to Billie Nelson while putting my wheels back in. I was using my thumbs to gauge the gaps either side of the swinging arm and he said: "Aren't you going to line the wheels up properly using string?" I said: "Nah, I don't bother with all that string and plank business like you do, I just do it by eye." Well, a bit later on I passed Billie coming out of Gerards Bend and he came over again afterwards and said: "I will never bother with that string malarkey ever again, it obviously doesn't make any ruddy difference!"

An all-star line-up at the 1968 post-TT meeting at Mallory Park includes Mike Hailwood, Percy Tait, Phil Read, Rod Gould, Ray Pickrell, Giacomo Agostini and Seeley-mounted John Cooper
(Mortons Archive)

12
12
4
24
47

On Colin Seeley's Matchless prototype, Brands Hatch, September 1967
(Nick Nicholls Collection, Mortons Archive)

Eyes right! John and Ago cross the start-finish line in the 1967 Race of the Year at Mallory Park. A rehearsal for things to come!
(Nick Nicholls Collection, Mortons Archive)

In the pack!
(Malcolm Carling Collection)

On the Seeley in 1969.
Yellow leathers by now
(Malcolm Carling Collection)

SWITCH TO SEELEY

John Cooper and Colin Seeley, a successful partnership
(Mortons Archive)

Turning in on the Seeley
(Malcolm Carling Collection)

Chris Carter: Your Nortons served you well but in the end you sold them and switched to Seeleys. In fact Seeleys were the bikes to have for a few years before the Japanese became completely dominant. What exactly were Seeleys?

I've still got the very first 500 Seeley ever made. Derek Minter rode it first, then John Blanchard, and then I was very successful on it.

In 1966 sidecar driver Colin Seeley started building his own solo frames fitted around AJS 7R and Matchless G50 engines in his workshop down in Kent. Derek Minter rode the first G50 prototype. It was competitive from the start but Derek was never that keen on it. When he left the team Blanchard was given the bike but he fell out with Colin at the 1967 TT. Later that year Colin retired from racing sidecars, bought out the AMC race shop and got serious about building solos full-time.

Meanwhile the Nortons were beginning to get a bit old-fashioned and less and less reliable. I was riding bikes that were six or seven years old and they were worn out really. They broke down no end of times, especially on the Isle of Man, but we had to just keep them going. Francis Beart's bikes were always very good on the Island because he only used them in the Manx Grand Prix and the TT so they never wore out.

There were one or two things coming along like the Paton and the QUB, and Triumph and Norton twins based on road bikes were another possibility. But then Colin asked me to ride his ex-Minter G50 prototype and I've still got it now. It's the first one Colin ever made and it's got a Matchless engine rather than a later Seeley one. They're pretty much the same, actually. Colin's wife used to work at Matchless and he used to have good contacts there and he could get engines from the factory.

Anyway, the time was right to sell my Nortons, and I sold four Manx Nortons in 1968 for £1000! Actually, I don't think the Matchless engine was any better than the Manx. It had similar characteristics in the way it made its power, but it was a particularly nice engine because it was clean and new, it didn't leak oil, and you could get brand new parts for it.

PADGETT YAMAHA

Chris Carter: At the same time, Japanese bikes started becoming available to privateers and they were coming into British road racing more and more. You rode for Padgetts, as I recall.

I was British 250cc champion in 1968 riding Yamaha TD1Cs for the Padgett brothers Peter and Don, from Batley in Yorkshire. I used to break lap records and win on their Yamaha twins although they were difficult, awful things to steer and hard to ride. Then they'd advertise and sell them with the line that this is the one that Cooper won on at Brands Hatch or wherever. Then they'd uncrate me another one.

They'd take 50% of my prize money too. At Mallory Park in October 1968, Peter said: "We're not tekkin' bike out o' van today 'cos tha's not paid up fer last two meetins." I said: "Funny you should say that, Peter, I've got an envelope in my van for you. I tell you what, I'd rather concentrate on the bigger classes anyway so that's fine, leave it in the van where it is." He said: "Well, that's a nice attitude! If you win today you'll be British Champion, doesn't that mean owt?"

I told him I wasn't particularly bothered, but I rode the bike eventually and wrapped up the championship. I also won the 500 and 350 events that day on Seeleys.

But boy, those TD1Cs were difficult to ride. When I rode for Padgetts at the TT that year we put about 4lb of lead wire around the frame to keep the front down, and I had a huge crash at the Ulster Grand Prix which put me in hospital for a week. I got into a big tank-slapper at Quarry Bends and lost it, hit a bank and knocked myself unconscious for four hours. When I came round, I had concussion for a while and they had to stitch up some bad gashes on my right hand and left arm.

RIGHT AND ABOVE RIGHT:
Cadwell Mountain action on the 250cc Padgett Yamaha. Leading Steve Machin (Bultaco) and Derek Chatterton respectively
Nick Nicholls Collection, Mortons Archive)

With Peter Padgett. Mallory Park paddock, October 1967
(Nick Nicholls Collection, Mortons Archive)

Padgett Yamaha TD1C
(Mortons Archive)

As John once famously said: "It's first under the linen that counts." (Mortons Archive)

Chris Carter: Now it's time to talk about the Yamsel, a bike that you created and on which you had incredible success. What's the story behind its development?

The Yamsel was a lightweight machine (Mortons Archive)

Colin Seeley made some really nice stuff. He was very fussy and his preparation was first class, and the Seeley 350 7R was a lovely bike in every way. Except that it wasn't fast enough.

The 350cc AJS 7R engine was getting on in years and becoming uncompetitive so Colin made a super-lightweight tubular frame for it. He used special Reynolds steel tubing and there were no downtubes at the front as the engine cases were used as part of the frame. I liked the Seeley 7R. All in all it was a very nice motorbike indeed. It steered well, braked well. In fact it did everything well except go fast, which was the problem Colin had set out to solve in the first place.

At the end of the 1960s Yamahas were starting to become the bike to have in the 250cc and 350cc classes, and although I was quite tall and Yamahas were made to suit Japanese riders who tended to be smaller than me, I thought, I've got to buy one of my own at some stage. I knew the speedway rider Barry Briggs and I asked him if he could get me a new 350 Yamaha from America. Barry arranged for one to be sent over, and when it arrived I put Dunlop tyres on it instead of Japanese Bridgestones and got it ready to take to a meeting at Cadwell Park. I took the 7R as well and thought I'll try both in practice and see how they compare. The Yamaha went like stink as I expected and the brakes were really good, but it didn't steer as well as the Seeley. I was rather scared of the Yamaha at first and I was wobbling around a bit, but even though I was much smoother on the 7R I decided to ride the Yamaha in the 350cc race. I thought if this is the future and I've got to make the change, it might as well be now.

But in the race I went round a long right-hand bend and then flicked left and it snapped back and flung me straight over the handlebars. I went flying head over heels and landed with a bang. The circuit owner Charlie Wilkinson was watching from that corner and I came to a stop right at his feet, scaring him half to death. Now as every rider will testify, Charlie was a man who never gave anything away but I shocked him so much that day by falling off so spectacularly in front of him that he gave me a hundred quid!

Anyway, I was pretty knocked about and there was no way I could drive home, so a racer called Steve Jolly kindly drove my van for me, and on the way back to Derby I lay in the back between the Yamaha and the Seeley 7R, wondering what my next move was going to be. I thought I've got one bike that handles beautifully but isn't competitive, and a Yamaha that's super-quick but doesn't steer well at all. Then it came to me. The answer was to put the Yamaha engine in the Seeley frame. Rodney Gould had put a Yamaha motor in a Bultaco frame but I went one better. The Seeley frame had no front downtubes and was perfect for the job.

When I got home I took the engine out of the Yamaha and blocked it up in the Seeley chassis. Then I rang Ron Herring up, who did Rodney's bike. His son used to be a scrambles rider and they lived in Brackley. I said: "If I bring this bike down with the engine bracketed in, would you help me design some downtubes for the frame?" He said: "Yes John, bring it down." So I took the bike to him in the van and he drew up some frame tubes. I took the drawings to Colin and he made them for me on the spot, then I went back to Ron who welded them in.

Back home again I carried on building the bike, sorting out the exhaust pipes and suchlike. I finished on a Friday lunchtime, and then tested it on Long Lane, the back road from Derby to Ashbourne. Straight away I thought: "Wow! This is a winner. I'm on to something special here." And I was right. Motorcycle design was as much guesswork as science in those days and by combining the best aspects of two very different bikes, I knew immediately I'd hit upon something really good.

The Yamsel, as I called it, was super-fast and it handled really well. I took it to a meeting at Mallory Park but it was a bit over-geared and Tony Rutter kept passing me down the straight. He beat me on the last lap but I knew what the problem was and I said to him afterwards: "You won't do that again Tony, I'll tell you that." And sure enough, I won 39 of the next 40 races I rode on it and I broke nearly every race and track record in the country.

I won the 1970 Race of the Year on it, which was quite something on a 350.

Chris Carter: **What was so good about it?**

The Yamsel was exceptionally quick. One of the reasons for that was there was a big gap between the carburettor bellmouths and the back mudguard. The Yamsel was five inches longer than an over-the-counter Yamaha which had its back mudguard close to the carburettors so the engine didn't breathe as well.

It also handled really well. My Yamsel was the same length as a Manx Norton which, as I've said, was considerably longer than a standard Yamaha of the time. The Yamahas were twitchy and prone to wobbling, whereas the Yamsel was stable. The Yamsel was also an exceptionally light and very basic bike. There were no air or choke levers on it or anything.

All I had on the bars was a clutch lever, a throttle and brake. No extra cables to worry about. It had a super-light frame and very narrow wheels which took a 3.18 front tyre and a 3.25 back, which was very small. Yamahas normally had 3.25 fronts and 3.50 rears and that was the trend at the time, but I went the opposite way.

Brands Hatch backwards on the 350 Yamsel, Hutchinson 100, August 1970 (Nick Nicholls Collection, Mortons Archive)

Leading the way at Scarborough in 1970 ahead of Steve Machin and a young Barry Sheene (Mortons Archive)

Getting ready to go. On the start-line, North West 200, 1970
(Mortons Archive)

John Cooper leads Tony Rutter and Barry Sheene, Brands Hatch, August 1971
(Nick Nicholls Collection, Mortons Archive)

Chris Carter: **Colin Seeley started making and selling Yamsels and there were replicas made by other people. Did you benefit financially from your invention?**

On the Yamsel I could win races for fun, beating people by half a lap, easy. I would sit behind them, pass them with two laps to go, then clear off and win by 200 yards. It was a fantastic bike and loads of people wanted them. In fact, Phil Read said he should've bought a Yamsel from me rather than make a copy which was never particularly good. Colin Seeley watched with interest and then he started making complete Yamsels and frame kits himself. He sold a good number in the end, although I never got anything out of it. Alan Barnett had one from Colin, so did Derek Chatterton and quite a few others

Cool, calm and collected. John on the Seeley at Scarborough
(Malcolm Carling Collection)

COLIN SEELEY

Constructor, race team owner and grand prix-winning sidecar racer

I've known John Cooper a long time and he is a bit of a special case. He has raced my bikes with great success and we're personal friends too. So I've seen both sides of him as a person and he's a good guy, to say the least. He's a kind and generous man who's always there to help people out.

He helped people throughout his career, people like Barry Sheene. Barry was a cocky and confident young man but without question he looked up to John and respected him a great deal. And John still helps people now. We've lost a lot of mutual friends over the years which is just the way of things, unfortunately.

I ring him up for a chat sometimes to make sure he's okay and quite often Rosie says he's gone out to see someone who's not very well or feeling down or in some sort of trouble. He follows it through. John's a smashing fellow but I don't want to sing his praises too much or it'll look over the top!

So I will say he can be bloody difficult sometimes and quite a critical person but then again, I can be too. We're similar in that way. We are both perfectionists in some respects and we have very high standards. We're sticklers for everything being right. I guess we took a liking to each other because we knew what we were talking about and we trusted each other to produce the goods. He enjoyed working with me and I with him. We are both fussy so-and-sos and we made a good team. And I must say John was never difficult to work with. If there were any problems he'd say so and we'd work together to put things right.

John was a terrific rider. So good you could almost say, what's he doing riding one of Colin Seeley's bikes! He did us a lot of good, there's no doubt about it, and I've always given him credit, but he's had a bit of a moan from time to time about the Yamsels, saying he didn't get a share of the profits I made from them. Well all I'll say is profit, what profit? I didn't make much out of them at all.

Anyway, John's always been smart in business, smarter than most people, and certainly smarter than me. He's still got his original garage premises where he used to do his MoTs and suchlike. He keeps hold of things, which is shrewd. He's still got the original prototype Seeley G50 which goes back to 1966, first ridden by Derek Minter, then John Blanchard, and then taken over by John with great success.

John was such a good rider. He could ride absolutely anything, and he was the first one to hang off the way he did. A great style. He wouldn't only be on his Seeley and his Yamsel, he'd be on other bikes at the same meeting and he'd win on them all. I know John was disappointed never to be offered a works ride. Top men, guys like Hailwood and Read, were world champions and John was right there with them, chasing them down, beating them on occasions, and knocking hard on the door. It was a shame the factory ride didn't come because he was quick, to say the least, and adaptable. He could ride any bike. He could have done a great job as a works rider and maybe even won a world championship.

Part of the problem was John never asked for favours and he's still like that today. He's quite shy, actually, and I've told him off over it from time to time. He won't ask for things.

And that was the problem back in the Sixties too. He didn't push himself forward. He didn't say: "Don't you know who I am? Give me that bike, I can beat anyone." Shout it from the rooftops. He just thought if they want me, they know where I am. Plain speaking, down to earth, no flannel. That's John. That's why he was loved by the fans, of course. That, and the fact he was always so approachable.

There was no real money around in the Sixties. When I got my first start money it was a fiver and I thought I'd arrived! There were plenty of entrants, people like the Arter brothers and Tom Kirby, but no real sponsorship beyond the trade. Racing was a serious business but it was fun at the same time.

It was a great period to be racing because there were lots of good guys all capable of beating each other. We didn't know who was going to win from one weekend to the next but we were all friends and we all respected each other. Racing was serious but we had a lot of fun too. We were mates.

Riders I've worked with in more recent years have not been so good at keeping in contact but people like Cooper, Dave Croxford and co, they've always kept in touch. Dave is a real character, he rang up recently and said: "Hi Col, I thought I'd give you a call to see if you're still alive!" Only Dave could do that. But the point is, he'd been thinking about me and wondering if I was okay. Riders from that era like John, Dave and myself still care about each other and we have a connection to this day.

too, and they all loved them. They were lovely lightweight bikes that steered very well indeed.

The Japanese frames got better over the years but nothing was quite as good as the Yamsel in its time, or certainly not better. It was a lovely bike but I maintain that if you're going to be successful with any bike, the first thing you need is a good rider. The best bike builders and tuners are invariably associated with good riders, I've always found.

ON RIDING

John Cooper in 1964: **"To get anywhere in racing you have to be cool, calm and collected, forgetting the opposition and moving forward at your own pace. There are times when something tells me I am going to win – but that doesn't mean I can take chances to do so."**

Chris Carter: Talk a little about a racer's mental attitude. What does it take to be a winning road racer?

To be a successful motorcycle racer you've got to have natural ability but it's about learning the trade as well. I was lucky in that I did seem to be naturally fast, but I worked at it too.

I remember when Derek Minter was right at the top of his game and I'd be right behind him and then all of a sudden he'd pull a gap and be 20 bike lengths in front and I'd think, how did he do that? So I'd claw my way back up to him and concentrate on what he was doing and learn how he did it. And I can remember when I first went to Brands Hatch I used to go up the left side of the road to the hairpin and cut across. But all the Brands Hatch scratchers used to go up the right side of the road, shudder to an almost complete stop and then make a tight turn so I couldn't get across, so I soon learned how to do it too.

They do the same at Mallory Park now. They go up the inside of the track, make a sharp turn, then accelerate out. They don't make a nice corner of it. With the slick tyres now you can do these things and they don't slip away but when we had treaded tyres with less grip we had to be a lot more careful. And nowadays they can go into corners sideways, sliding the bikes under full control, which we couldn't do on the tyres we had in our time.

But if you can ride, you can ride and I was always competitive, particularly on short circuits on 250s, 350s and 500s. Some days I didn't feel like it as much as others I suppose but I worked up to it and by the time practising was over and the racing started I was ready to go. You had to be

Riding a motorbike properly. At Mallory Park in 1965, heading for a win on the 246cc Greeves
(Mortons Archive)

really. I was fortunate in that I was often the bloke to beat. I was psychologically strong. I knew I could do it.

All through my career I had a name for being good at Mallory Park but I never had a favourite track. I used to think if you're going to be a professional motorbike racer you've got to go well everywhere, and if you don't like a place you've got to get to like it. I gradually became good at all of them.

I won a lot of races at Mallory Park and I was always fast round Gerards and through the Esses, but I won plenty of races at lots of other places too – Oulton Park, Scarborough and Aberdare Park, for example. Brands Hatch took longer to crack. I didn't get my first Brands win until 1964 but many more followed. I also won races in Holland, Italy and the US. It's all about being able to ride a motorbike properly, isn't it?

I held the lap record at Aberdare Park, and I beat Mike Hailwood there on my 350 Gold Star in a Manx frame. He was on a Norton, which was faster, but I was quicker at the Esses and other places. I went back a few years ago when they had a meeting to raise funds for the wife of a lad who got killed in the Isle of Man. I rode my Seeley and afterwards Bob Heath said: "Do you know John, you ride over the same bit of tarmac every lap and you're hardly any slower now than you used to be." I said: "Believe me, Bob, I am going slower, but yes, I do remember the lines."

I never trained or did anything like that but I was talking to Chris Walker a while back and he said: "In the 1960s there was a meeting virtually every weekend and you were riding three or four races every time. That in itself kept you fit." There's something in that. Concentration is another key thing. Like everyone else, my mind would drift sometimes to mundane things or reflect on something I'd read or been speaking about earlier. It's strange how the mind works.

I didn't think much about danger but I will say some of the very fast circuits where we were doing 130 or 140mph could be difficult. The Belgian Grand Prix at Spa, for example. Stavelot on a Norton was absolutely flat out an inch or two from the kerb and a slight mistake would likely mean death and sometimes I'd think: "Wow! That was close." At the old Sachsenring Peter Williams was in front of me and we were going at well over 100mph and he went off the track on a right-hand bend and went down a ditch. Bang! Big crash which nearly killed him. He was lucky to get away with that one.

But lots of things are dangerous. I've done aerobatics in light aircraft and that's dangerous. You have to acknowledge risk but if you go around all the time thinking motorcycle racing is dangerous you'll never win anything, that's for sure. I had some accidents obviously, but I always rode a little bit within myself and I was always pretty careful. If somebody was going a lot faster than I was comfortable with, I was prepared to let them go. You've got to respect the conditions, and know your limitations and the limits of the bike. If I ever came across anyone who was a bit wild, it was always best to get past them and clear off. Beat them. No point in talking to them about the error of their ways.

Some people say you can't be good on both a two-stroke and a four-stroke or you can't be good on big bikes and little 'uns but some riders could and in 1985 Freddie Spencer won two world championships in a year, 250cc and 500cc. In my opinion, if you can ride a motorbike you can ride anything. We used to ride 250, 350 and 500cc machines in a day and sometimes even a 125 and think nothing of it. I used to ride a two-stroke 250 Yamaha twin and a 500 Norton single on the same afternoon, and I won on that evil-handling BSA and on a Domiracer I'd never sat on before.

Bespectacled superstars John Cooper and Peter Williams. Peter was an early adopter of the full-face helmet
(Malcolm Carling Collection)

On the Seeley, scrapping with Norton-mounted Tony Jefferies
(Malcolm Carling Collection)

NEIL TUXWORTH

Racer and manager of Honda Racing from 1989 to 2017

My very earliest memory of John Cooper dates back to my schoolboy years when I saw him win a very wet 350cc International race at Cadwell Park. He lapped nearly the entire field and I just could not believe how fast he was compared to the other top riders that day. That impression has always stuck firmly in my mind. Over the next few years I had the pleasure of watching John win many more races at both national and international level at many different circuits around the UK.

I began my own racing career in 1969 and in the early 1970s I was often competing in the same races as John, although he was a far better rider than me and I didn't see much of him as he disappeared off into the distance. During this time I got to know him a little and we gradually built up a friendship.

One of my most memorable races from those days was the 350cc event at the Race of Aces international meeting at Snetterton. I was alongside John throughout the whole race and we changed positions many times with John eventually finishing fifth and me sixth. I was at the peak of my powers then and John was by then perhaps a little past his absolute best, so in no way does it mean I could ever be compared to him as a rider. But it did give me a great feeling of satisfaction to have been able to race wheel to wheel with John Cooper on at least one occasion in my career!

In my opinion John Cooper was one of the greatest British riders ever, capable on his day of beating people like Derek Minter, Mike Hailwood, Bill Ivy and Phil Read. If John had been on the same level of machinery as some of these riders, I have no doubt whatsoever he could have been a world champion. John won several British championships and many international races around the world, and who will ever forget the day he beat Agostini in the Race of the Year at Mallory Park? John was not everyone's 'cup of tea', so to speak, because he always said what he thought and this sometimes upset people, but I have always admired him for his forthright views.

I also believe many top riders feared John Cooper and knew they could not beat him on equal machinery.

After John retired I got to know him much better and I now count him as a good friend. But more than this, I still look up to him as a great rider. When John takes part in a classic parade he is still quick, but always sensible and steady and sometimes when I watch other riders from his heyday go flying past him I can imagine what he must be thinking.

He has absolutely nothing to prove to them or anyone else and if the clock was put back none of those riders would get anywhere near him. John Cooper simply was one of the greatest British riders in history and I am so proud to count him as one of my true friends.

Man and machine in perfect harmony. John and his Yamsel at Mallory Park. Steve Machin leads the pursuit
(Nick Nicholls Collection, Mortons Archive)

LEATHERS AND HELMETS

Chris Carter: Coloured leathers came in at the end of the 1960s and you were an early adopter. Talk a little about the gear you wore.

Throughout the Sixties we all wore thin leathers, gloves and boots, all with very little reinforcement and no armour. And we wore pudding basin helmets with leather straps that covered our ears. Around the time of the Yamsel in 1970 I started wearing coloured leathers and I was one of the first. My speedway friend Nigel Boocock had used blue leathers for a while – they called him Little Boy Blue – and he suggested I got some coloured leathers. I had some yellow ones made first, and then a blue set like Nigel's.

I endorsed Lewis Leathers' boots. I wore their standard boots and suggested a few modifications which they took on board, and after that they brought out a design they called John Cooper racing boots. I went down to London a year or two back and bought a pair of the same boots. They still make them!

With spectacles under goggles, steaming up could sometimes be a problem in the wet. In the 1964 Ulster Grand Prix I stopped three times to change my goggles and eventually had to retire as I just couldn't see.

But on a motorbike I need to feel the wind on my face and that's how it should be. When I rode at Ontario in America I took my pudding basin helmet but Bell asked me to ride with one of their open-face jet designs.

They fitted me up with one, painted it and put moon eyes on the front and number 28 on the side. I've still got it now. They also gave me a full-face helmet to try but I just can't ride in them. I can't stand the claustrophobic feeling I get when I wear them. Arai gave me one a while back and I tried it on my road bike, but it threw me completely. I was getting my left and right mixed up on the foot controls. But I like my half-face Arai with a wrap-around visor.

NORMAN STORER

Chris Carter: Norman Storer is someone we've both known since childhood, and he's also an incredibly gifted motorcyclist. Tell us about him.

Norman Storer was probably the best all-round motorcyclist Britain's ever had. He was extremely talented but he was never particularly ambitious and he never promoted himself. He's also a very good friend of mine and when he finally stopped racing he ended up working for me for 10 years.

Norman's about six years older than me and I first came across him when I was a lad and used to watch scrambling. He used to whip round Clifton, Muggington and Turnditch and I think he could have been a motocross world champion if he'd stuck with it. He was also a superb trials rider. One day he got a hopeless wreck of a Royal Enfield trials bike out of the motorcycle shop where he worked, rode it in the Bemrose Trial and finished about fourth. He rode in trials all over the place and won a first class award at the Scottish Six Days Trial.

A star rider in scrambles and trials, he was damn good at grass track racing as well, and then he went road racing and

SPEEDWAY

Chris Carter: I've been a track announcer at speedway and I've always enjoyed watching it and spending time with riders. But it's a sport not too many road racing fans know much about.

I started going to speedway in around 1950. It was a night out. I used to go to Long Eaton on my bicycle when I was a boy, and later on a motorbike. There were huge crowds at speedway after the war and it's been popular again at various times since, but you never see a policeman at a speedway track. There's never any trouble. The people who go are nice people. Whole families go along with their scarves and their rattles. They all buy a programme and fill them in on the terraces.

I was godfather to Nigel Boocock's son, Darren, and I used to go along to Sheffield Speedway with him and meet up with Nigel's brother Eric, another former rider, and have a meal in the restaurant there before the meeting. But then Darren and his wife were killed in a road bike crash and I haven't been back since. When Darren died his dad never really got over it and he started drinking heavily. He died a few years ago.

In the pits with Nigel Boocock
(Mortons Archive)

Nigel was a nice lad and a good rider. He had the potential to be a world champion but on very big nights he'd get terribly nervous and he had some big crashes and banged his head a few times. I used to go along as his mechanic sometimes and on occasion riders would come up to him in the pits and say: "Will you sell me some points Nigel? If you let me beat you in the next race I'll give you a couple of hundred quid." And he would. Ridiculous.

New Zealander Ivan Mauger was the most successful rider of Nigel and Norman Storer's era and for a while afterwards, winning six world finals. There were better riders out there at various times but Mauger was so good at getting out of the gate, sliding it around the middle of the track and cutting the corners off, that it was difficult for anyone to pass him. He used to make a flying start and he knew how to block the track up so nobody could get past.

The multi-talented Norman Storer at Alton Towers in 1956
(John Cooper Collection)

he was brilliant at that too. But he fell off and broke his wrists and that was the end of him as a competitive road racer. His scaphoids were just too painful after that and there was nothing that could be done about it. I think surgery can help these days, but at the time that was not the case.

Norman rode a works Greeves scrambler for a while and Bert Greeves' cousin Derry Preston-Cobb wanted Norman to go on the continent and ride in the European Motocross Championship but he was more interested in road racing at the time and didn't want to give that up, so he turned the offer down. Almost immediately Brian Stonebridge, who would have been his team-mate, was killed in a road accident while on Greeves business, and almost certainly Norman would have been in the car with him that day.

Sometime in 1963 I said to Norman: "I'm going to Long Eaton Speedway tonight, do you want to come with me?" He said he'd never been to a speedway match before but he'd come along. We went the next week too and during the meeting he said: "I wouldn't mind having a go at this." So I took him to see the promoters, Ron Wilson and Reg Fearman, and asked if he could have a try-out if I found him a bike. I said: "I'll tell you something now, I'll bet he'll end up riding for you." Ron wasn't impressed. "We've heard all that before," he said, "but sure, he can have a ride."

The next day I rang Tommy Price up at his workshop in London. Tommy was a retired Wembley Lions speedway rider and former world champion who was dabbling in road racing at the time. I explained the situation and Tom offered to lend us a bike. So we went down and picked it up and for a couple of weeks Norman practised on the track after the meetings, and then he rode in the second half of the meeting, i.e., in proper races but not part of a league match. Of course, he was competitive straight away and the next week he went straight into the team and he rode professional speedway for many years for Long Eaton and Leicester, finally retiring in 1975.

NORTH WEST 200

Chris Carter: **You've mentioned the North West 200 in Northern Ireland a couple of times. It's a race meeting that's still held today. Tell us more about your experiences there.**

The old North West 200 was one hell of a circuit and unbelievably fast. You used to go down to the seafront, turn left and along the coast road to Coleraine flat out for about four miles. It was downhill at the end and we ran huge sprockets for really high gearing. On my Seeley one day I was clocked at 157mph. I was probably slipstreaming somebody to do that but by God, it was fast along there.

The last time that circuit was used was 1971 and I won the 500cc race in torrential rain; mind you, it always seemed to rain at the North West. That year it was absolutely thumping it down all day long and I got so wet through in the 350 race and I was so miserable and freezing cold I wasn't going to ride in the 500 event, even though I'd won it the previous year.

My leathers were saturated, I was shivering with cold and my teeth were chattering, and in those conditions my specs would steam up during a race and my goggles too. I really didn't fancy another eight very long laps of it, but Robin Miller, the editor of Motor Cycle News, started my van up and got the heater going, and we sat chatting together in the cab for a bit while the rain drummed on the roof and washed down the windscreen. It cheered me up and thawed me out enough to feel that I would have a go after all and I went out and won the 500 race in pouring rain.

When I came back we weighed my leathers and there was 7lb of water in them! And wouldn't you know it, as soon as racing was over, the weather broke and the bloody sun came out!

I was just behind Tommy Robb in the

On the Yamsel at the North West 200, screen smashed by flying debris from Tommy Robb's big crash earlier in the race (Malcolm Carling Collection)

6

350 race at the North West one year and as he tried to pass someone the chap drifted out. Tommy clipped the kerb and went over the handlebars. It was a huge accident. His bike hit some railings and the forks ripped off, and they came flying back over, missing my head by a fraction as I ducked down and smashing my Yamsel's screen to pieces.

Geoff Barry was a lad from Derbyshire and I used to loan him my bikes occasionally to help him out. I got him a ride in the North West 200 one time and tried to help him get a good result. He used to run on the right-hand side of the bike on push starts which always looked clumsy, and he never seemed to get a good start. I said: "If I get a good start, Geoff, I'll go nice and steady over Shell Bridge and round the slow, early corners and hold everyone up, then you can go steaming down the outside and get into the lead, and clear off. I'll catch you up later."

Well, the plan worked a treat and after a few laps he was a good way in front and I was baulking all-comers behind him. Then we came to the last lap and I closed up right behind him, but then we came across a back-marker. Geoff went up the inside of him but it sadly it was the wrong choice. The guy turned across Geoff and slowed him up, and I rode round the outside and won. And when we got back to the paddock the cheeky bastard said: "You were lucky there John, if it hadn't been for that back marker you'd never have beaten me."

Sadly Geoff was one of those riders who had an extremely high opinion of himself, when actually he was not quite as good as he thought he was. He got killed in 1977 in the Killinchy 150 road races at Dundrod in Ireland. Ron Haslam was behind him at the time and he said Geoff was out of control nearly all the time, yet he kept looking round and signalling for Ron to get behind him. Ron kept his distance and Geoff eventually crashed and broke his neck. Only a fortnight before that he'd left his job to go racing full-time. He had a really good job working for Rolls-Royce on their nuclear programme. There was no way he should have turned professional. He was a nice lad but he rode beyond his limits.

I've seen it before and since, and thought it can't go on like this. I said to Steve Henshaw once in the Isle of Man, you're falling off too much Steve, why don't you pack it in? Valerie, his wife, is such a nice girl and she backed me up, but of course he didn't listen and the worst happened. He was such a nice lad and it was very sad.

John getting soaking wet at the North West 200. Note the street furniture!
(Malcolm Carling Collection)

McINTYRE
THE BABY SHOP
21

Full concentration
(Mortons Archive)

John Cooper, MCN Man of the Year 1970

Clash of the greats at Mallory Park

Cooper quote: 'I was never under pressure; it was no trouble at all, youth'

CAREFREE COOPER WINS A THOUSAND GUINEAS

report: JOHN BROWN

pictures: MALCOLM CARLING

RACE OF THE YEAR RESULTS

THE WRONG PRAYER

New Competition Kits from Stock

COMERFORDS

1970

Race of the Year

Gary Nixon, Mallory Park race of the Year, 1970: "Cooper? Oh he's just perfect, just perfect. A great ride."

Come on lads, keep up! (Mortons Archive)

A flawless performance (Mortons Archive)

A reflective moment at Tilburg in the Netherlands, a happy hunting ground for John over many years (Jan Burgers)

John Cooper on the BSA triple with Percy Tait and Ray Pickrell, Mallory Park, April 1971
(Nick Nicholls Collection, Mortons Archive)

BSA 750 TRIPLE

Chris Carter: The final phase of your career was highly successful and you'll be forever associated with the BSA triple on which you had some really big wins.

I went well enough on the 500 Seeley Matchless but when I got on board the three-cylinder BSA 750 I went from strength to strength and got some really big results that I'm remembered for to this day. It all started when someone from BSA-Triumph rang me up one day in early 1971 and said: "We're short of a rider for the Transatlantic Match Races, would you be interested in riding a factory triple? We've got a spare bike in bits under the bench." They built it up and Percy Tait, who was a Triumph test rider for many years, told me it was a virtually standard bike, no special head or pistons or anything like that, but it went really well. I liked it. It was light, it had a nice clutch on it. I rode it in the Match Races against the Americans and I scored quite well, and then it went back to the BSA factory.

I can remember Gary Nixon was in the US team for that first Match Race series. I'd met him the previous year when he came to Mallory Park for the Race of the Year and in practice he was going round Gerards putting his foot out, trying to slide it! I said: "That's not how to do it Gary." He eventually got the hang of it. He was a good lad. I liked him and we became good friends.

Chris Carter: The triple was basically a road bike. Did it have a standard frame?

The standard triple was okay as the basis of a racing bike but the handling needed improvement so they got Rob North to make a frame. It wasn't all that good to begin with but Percy made various recommendations and when Rob made some adjustments it became very good indeed. Later on, when I rode the triple at the Ontario Speedway in California, Rob North was there and he mentioned that he wouldn't mind living and working over there full-time. Later on I mentioned Rob to some people out there and he ended up getting a job. He hasn't been back since.

RACE OF THE YEAR

Chris Carter: Now we come to an important chapter in the John Cooper story, your victory over Giacomo Agostini in the 1971 Race of the Year at Mallory Park. According to legend you had to persuade the BSA factory to give you a bike and to do that you promised to win the race.

The 1971 Race of the Year at Mallory Park has gone down as one of the great motorcycle races of all time
(Artwork: John Hancox)

I won the 1970 Race of the Year on my 350 Yamsel, beating Phil Read just as I had done in 1965, although to be fair Phil was on his 250 after his 350 broke its crank in an earlier race. I was keen to win it again in 1971 but to do so I needed to get back on a factory triple. When I won the Race of the Year in 1971 I filled Mallory Park. As many as 65,000 people were there, and a lot of them were literally bussed in. There hasn't been a crowd as big as that before or since and a lot of them came specifically because I was quoted in MCN saying I was going to win on the triple. I said to Peter Deverall, the marketing director at BSA: "If you lend me that motorbike I'll win the Race of the Year for you."

Chief engineer Doug Hele had previously told me there was no bike available. He said: "Sorry John, but we've got Percy Tait, we've got Ray Pickrell and we've got Tony Jefferies." But Peter Deverall had a word and Doug said: "Okay John, come over and see me." I did that and then Doug said: "Let's go to Mallory Park and you can have a test." I said: "What's the point of that? I've already ridden the BSA there in the Match Races so you know how well I can go." Anyway, he insisted, so we went and I broke the lap record three times and when I pulled in he said: "How did you find the short cut?"

Before the Race of the Year I went to Scarborough and had four wins. I think I was the first man to do that at an international meeting there. I always went well at Scarborough but that was exceptional, so I guess I was in good form. I certainly felt confident and at Mallory Park I won the 1000cc event earlier in the weekend, beating Gary Nixon.

There was a strong line-up for the 1971 Race of the Year. Mike Hailwood had entered on a 350cc Yamaha, Giacomo Agostini was there on his 500cc factory MV Agusta and the flying Finn Jarno Saarinen had come across too. Barry Sheene was leading the 125cc world championship at the time. He was also in the field, and Gary Nixon was over from the States and ended up riding a 350 Yamaha lent to him by Barry. And I lent Phil Read my Yamsel, I recall. As you can see we all helped each other quite a bit in those days. Also in the field were people like Paul Smart, Tony Rutter, Derek Chatterton and Steve Machin.

It was a strong entry, and because Agostini was there and because I'd been widely quoted in the motorcycle press saying I was going to win, the atmosphere was absolutely electric all day. At that time clutch starts were coming in. For years we never used to do clutch starts at all, it was always push starts. On the day the clerk of the course Arthur Taylor, in his wisdom, said he'd like to make the Race of the Year a clutch start but he need to get agreement on this from all the riders because in the regulations it was down as a race with a push start. So he asked us all and the only person who wouldn't agree to it was Agostini because the MV was light and easy to push. Of course, the BSA triple was a heavy bike and harder to start.

Chris Carter: Tell us about the race itself.

On the line I pushed for all I was worth and I could hear engines firing all around me. I gave it a few more steps and then dropped on the seat and the BSA went first time. I thought: "Bloody hell, that was lucky." I was about fourth at the end of the first lap, but I got through and caught Agostini and got past him. But he got back in front going into the hairpin and then I had a big slide at the Esses which dropped me back a bit. I caught him up once again and passed him with three laps to go. I got my head down, kept it smooth and opened up a bit of a gap, and I ended up winning the race by about half a second. Ray Pickrell was third, but a long way back.

It was most satisfying to say I'd win the race, then carry out my promise. And when I passed Agostini going into the Esses I heard the crowd cheer, and I could hear them at the hairpin too and see the programmes waving around the circuit. How many racers have ever experienced that? Even today people are always coming up to me and saying: "I was there on the big day, you know." It was a big event and people were chuffed to have seen me do it. The fans went home happy, especially the ones with moon eyes on their own helmets. It was a lovely day. Ago was the baddie because he was a foreigner and I was the hero because I was a local lad on a British bike. It had all the ingredients.

Colin Seeley: **"Since Hailwood and Honda had quit the grand prix scene back in 1967 the 1971 Race of the Year was the first time Agostini had been beaten in a straight fight."**

Chris Carter: How did the BSA compare with the works MV? Did Ago have an advantage, or did you?

It was hard work beating Agostini, but part of the reason why I did it was because the BSA was so good from low revs, I could let the clutch out and drive round the hairpin and away while Ago was having to keep the revs up and slip the clutch. I gained 10 or 12 yards each lap that way, which was just enough to cancel out the MV's speed advantage around the rest of the circuit. That and the fact I was a bit faster coming out of Gerards and through the Esses.

I was on a 750 and he was on a 500 so I had a 250cc advantage, but then again the BSA was basically a road bike with a pushrod engine and the MV was a hand-built grand prix machine so we were fairly evenly matched. All in all, it was a combination of a bit of luck and a bit of skill. And I had to work hard for it. Ago was a top, top rider.

The Race of the Year, Mallory Park, 19 September, 1971
(Malcolm Carling Collection / Mortons Archive)

BSA Rocket 3
LOCKHEED
DUNLOP
1971
Race of the Year

On the way to another win over Ago at the Brands Hatch Race of the South
(Nick Nicholls Collection, Mortons Archive)

Chris Carter: The Race of the South was another big international meeting. It was held the following weekend and you were up against Ago once again.

When I beat Ago I was the first person to do it for years and some people said: "Well, it's only Mallory Park. How hard was he trying?" Well, I'll tell you this: Ago wanted to win that race. A couple of weeks later we were both at Brands Hatch for the Race of the South and he said: "I've got a new engine." I said: "Funny you should say that but so have I." I beat him there as well, and on another occasion at Cadwell Park.

Of course they are all short circuits, but the way I looked at it, a grand prix track was just like two or three short circuits joined together. There are only so many combinations and types of corner and I was comfortable racing anywhere.

In the Race of the South, Ago got away first but I passed him at Druids, then pulled away to win. And I broke Mike Hailwood's outright lap record. After that BSA started thinking about sending me to Ontario, California to take part in the Champion Spark Plugs Classic.

After the Race of the South I gave the Irish singer Clodagh Rodgers a ride around the circuit. She was reckoned to have the best legs in show business at the time and her voice was insured for £1 million. She was at the height of her fame but she was good fun.

She said she'd like to go round the track and so I said: "Jump on the back then!" and off we went. Someone shouted out: "Crash helmets!" but I said "Bugger that," under my breath and ignored him. When we got back she said she'd really enjoyed it.

Hang on tight, love! A lap of honour with Clodagh Rogers, Brands Hatch, October 1971
(Unknown)

I first saw John in action one race day morning many, many moons ago at Mallory Park. He was scorching around at damn near unbeatable speeds on his Yamsel and his trusty Seeley G50. It seems he was having a lookie at me too, in between his practices. Later in the paddock I suddenly heard: "Ey up youth, 'ow you gerrin on round 'ere?" It was of course the lanky lad himself. I was over at Padgett's van, where I was watching Peter setting the ignition timing on John's TR2 Yamsel with an electronic beeper, which zeeeeeed up whenever the points broke contact.

I told John that I had watched him into Gerards and he seemed to be 15mph faster than most, the same at the Esses and Devil's Elbow! He smiled and looked rather embarrassed, and then he went on in great detail about how he did it. He explained that it wasn't the going in, but the half-way through and the exits which gave him the launch down Stebbe straight, and then he carried that speed around the Esses and up the hill to the hairpin. "Always oop the inside youth, never on the outside cutting in!" Of course, I was extremely thankful for

RACING'S BIGGEST PRIZE

Chris Carter: You mentioned BSA were considering sending you to race at the new Ontario Motor Speedway track in the US.

In October 1971 after winning the Race of the Year and the Race of the South at Brands Hatch, the BSA factory flew me over me to California for the Champion Spark Plugs Classic at Ontario. It was a marathon 250-mile race held over two legs with a 45-minute break in between to make adjustments and change tyres. That would be exhausting enough, but the weather was absolutely red hot.

The first leg started badly. I was sitting there on the start-line in neutral and as soon as the flag marshal lifted his flag they all went, literally leaving me standing. I was waiting for him to bring it down! So I was about 20th on the first lap and lucky not to have been taken out, but I got going and carved my way through, eventually finishing third. The track was like Daytona, fast with steep banking, and I was clocked at 165mph on the BSA.

In the second leg someone blew an engine up and a lot of blokes went down on the oil. I went wide and avoided it and went into the lead. I was leading the race for ages and got a bit bored and fed up to be honest. Eventually Kel Carruthers caught me and I let him through to make it more interesting because I knew I could pass him whenever I wanted.

But because Gary Nixon and some of the other BSA riders had fallen off on the oil, my mechanics were helping their mechanics trying to get them back into the race, and as a result of this I wasn't getting any pit signals. But that was okay because there was a big control tower in the middle of the track with a scoreboard on it which displayed the number of laps left to go. I was looking at this and when it finally indicated there were two laps remaining I thought: "Right, I'll get a move on and catch Kel up now," but when we went across the start-line soon afterwards the last lap flag was out. Obviously the scoreboard operator was being a bit slow changing the numbers over. I thought: "Bloody hell, I've left it too late."

But what the heck, I gave it a go anyway. It was a bit chaotic as we were lapping so many people but I closed up on Kel and when we flashed past the pit lane I was right up behind him.

And between there and the finishing line, a distance of about half a mile, I managed to pull out of Kel's slipstream and I won the race by about four inches – the length of a spark plug in fact! I not only won the second leg, but took the overall winner's prize as well. I got $15,000 for my day's work and poor old Kel got just $6000. His wife Jan had been signalling for him in the pits and when I got to the winners' rostrum and went up on the top step she said: "What are you doing up there?" I said: "I won it, Jan." She said: "You bloody Pommie bastard!" It took her a while to forgive me for that.

And when I'd received the trophy and I stood there garlanded with flowers, I was joined on the podium by Doug Hele. Recognising that I'd won the Race of the Year, the Race of the South and the richest race in the world over just a few weeks, he turned to me and said: "I suppose I've got to admit, you're not a bad rider." I said: "Well that's very kind of you Doug, thank you very much!" And then I collected my nice Heuer watch and my cheque for $15,000, which was a tremendous amount of money at the time. I received them, incidentally, from another John Cooper. Not the racing driver, but the Ontario circuit manager.

On the long flight home I was sitting next to an American guy who was knowledgeable about motorcycles. I enjoyed his company and we talked about bikes all the way back to England. I didn't think anything more about it until a few weeks later when the film The Great Escape came on the TV at home. Hang on a minute, I thought. I know that bloke. It was only then that the penny dropped and I realised I'd been chatting away for hours with Steve McQueen.

My wife Rosemary laughs about this but she's got no room to talk. We were in a department store in the States a few years ago and she fell into conversation with a glamorous and sophisticated black lady. It was only when the lady went to leave that we noticed the flunky carrying her shopping, and then as we all stepped outside a limousine swished to a halt to collect her. Right on cue I opened the door and she stepped straight in just like royalty. Who was this impressive person? None other than Diana Ross.

ALEX GEORGE

Grand Prix rider and three-time Isle of Man TT winner

[t]his wisdom and advice from this warm [a]nd friendly fellah, who was at that time [t]he absolute STAR in English racing. He [f]inished up by saying he was going down [t]o Gerards after his race to have a look [a]t my heat. I felt honoured that he was [i]nterested in youngsters coming through [l]ike me, I was after all 'Scottish Champ' at [t]he time.

My heat came. It was a run and bump start and of course the bloody thing did not start straight away and I got away midfield. To cut a long story short, using [J]ohn's advice I cut through the field and finished fifth, I think. Back I came into the paddock feeling quite proud of myself. [J]ohn appeared at the van looking well upset. He whacked me around the ear and said: "You were the fastest man going round but you were 30 bloody seconds behind the leaders!" I got the point: work on starting otherwise his mentoring would mean nothing!

That was the calibre of the man. Later he let us use his workshops in Chandos [P]ole Street in Derby and he was always ready to share advice and ideas whenever he was around. A gentle soft-spoken man off-bike, but God help you if you were in front of him on the track because he would out-think and outride you. John was a born winner and an approachable superstar loved and adored by his fans.

I was at Mallory again when he took on and beat, fair and square, the handsome Giacomo Agostini and his mighty 500cc MV triple. You could not see a blade of grass anywhere, there were so many screaming fans packed around the circuit, and it was jam-packed in the paddock too. He treated us all to a riding masterclass.

John was quicker into and around Gerards, while the MV had more top end power down the straights. The sight of John almost flat on his side, on full power-slide mode on the BSA out of Devil's Elbow, still sends chills down me. With move and counter move, they battled for, I believe, 30 laps and the drama included a lock-to-lock, potentially career-ending near highside for John on the BSA. John had a huge photo of it on his office wall and when I asked him about it once over a brew, he calmly described it as "just a moment"!!!

As we all know John won that mega race and he has received God-like adoration as a result. It was surely one of the best, if not THE best race ever seen at Mallory Park. To this day John remains matter-of-fact about his superb racing exploits. He has scratched round with the best of them and WON, beating Hailwood, Ago, Readie, Croxford, Barnett, Dunphy, Minter, Randle, Rutter, et al... I and many others, hold the man in high regard both on and certainly off a bike. These days he indulges his spanners-on skills restoring and riding his classic loves, and long may it continue. He has also established himself as a popular ambassador for our beloved sport and he is active in many charity events. We were together just recently at a National Motorcycle Museum open day. The place was full and as always John was there, sharing stories and memories with the fans. A brilliant rider, and a great friend and mentor, I certainly would not have reached the heights I did without his counsel.

Thank you 'Moon Eyes'.

BSA No.1 AGAIN
B.S.A. with John Cooper riding a Rocket 3 continues its fantastic series of race victories by beating the cream of world riders and machines to win the Ontario 'California' 250 mile classic.
1. J. COOPER BSA Rocket 3.
2. K. CARRUTHERS Yamaha
3. R. GRANT Suzuki
4. D. SMITH Yamaha
also 6th J. RICE BSA and 9th R. MANN BSA
(subject to official confirmation)
BSA race successes in 1970 and 1971
1st and 3rd at Daytona, March 1971
1st, 2nd and 3rd in Trans A.M.A. Moto Cross Championship, 1970
1st in BBC TV Grandstand Scramble Series, 1970
1st in ITV World of Sport Scramble Series, 1970
French 10 km Standing Start Record 1970 — 184.049 k.p.h.
BSA
BSA Motor Cycles Ltd., Armoury Road, Birmingham B11 2PX. Telephone: 021-772 2381
CHAMPION
SPARK PLUGS
DEPENDABLE
HEUER
CHRONOGRAPH
BSA
Cycle
BSA Roc
DUNLOP

Ontario Classic

Winning racing's richest prize: the Champion Spark Plugs Classic at the Ontario Motor Speedway, California, USA in October 1971 (Dave Friedman (Don Emde Collection) / Mortons Archive)

(Howard Allen.)

(Dave Friedman (Don Emde Collection)

On the BSA triple ahead of Ray Pickrell (Triumph) and Cal Rayborn (Harley Davidson), Oulton Park, Easter 1972
(Mortons Archive)

MAN OF THE YEAR

Chris Carter: And the prizes kept coming in 1971, even after the season had finished.

Motor Cycle News Man of the Year was an award voted for by MCN readers. I won it three times altogether including back-to-back wins in 1970 and 1971. I appreciated it very much.

It was nice to be popular with the fans and the plus for MCN was they could put their logo on the winner's bike for a year.

It's not such a big deal these days but years ago it was considered quite significant and prestigious.

In those days MCN sold around 180,000 copies a week and they plugged the competition hard over two or three weeks.

A huge number of voting coupons were sent in and that particular year I won easily.

Beating Ago twice and winning in America was a huge thing and in 1971 I got more votes than all the other entries put together.

FALLING TO EARTH

Chris Carter: What happened next?

After the successes of 1971 things went downhill a little bit, although I rode the BSA as a privateer the following year and won quite a few races and I was the first ever MCN British Superbikes champion. But BSA-Triumph was in trouble and in 1972 the factory decided not to run a works team.

Instead they loaned bikes to riders with very limited support. In my case they just paid for mechanic Steve Brown to prepare the bike for me at my garage at Chandos Pole Street.

I gave the TT a miss on the triple that year. If BSA-Triumph had a proper team I would have had a go but as it was, it was much too expensive. I said at the time: "I might break down and have nothing to show for it except a hole in my wallet."

But at the end of 1972 BSA got the cheque book out for a final time and I went back to Ontario at the company's expense. They paid for me to go to Las Vegas for three days, flew me to the track in a private aircraft and put me up in a nice hotel. It was all really kind of them but sadly I didn't stand any chance of winning the event a second time. The tyres Dunlop took were far too hard and even though I was the highest finisher in the team it was absolutely hopeless. I couldn't even keep up with Phil Read on the John Player Norton, that's how bad they were!

And at the end of the year the factory announced it was withdrawing from racing completely and the bike had to go back. I said at the time it had done 600 miles without a major overhaul and it was 'going like a jewel'. Riding a motorbike properly is partly about sensing what's hurting the thing and how far you can go. Some people are really hard on bikes, when I rode the BSA I used to rev it to about 8400 to 8500rpm and I think Percy Tait and Ray Pickrell were taking them up to 9000. I always had higher gearing which suited me and I didn't break down on it once.

John Cooper (BSA) and Peter Williams (Norton), Brands Hatch, August 1972
(Nick Nicholls Collection, Mortons Archive)

FAR RIGHT:
Return to Ontario, 1972: Phil Read and Peter Williams on John Player Nortons also in the picture
(Dave Friedman (Don Emde Collection))

More Match Race action. John Cooper ahead of Ray Pickrell and Tony Jefferies (right)
(Nick Nicholls Collection, Mortons Archive)

Chris Carter: **You've just been taking the Mickey out of John Player Norton but you ended up riding for them. Explanation please!**

John Player Norton boss Frank Perris had been after me to ride for them for a while and in the end NVT chairman Dennis Poore asked me personally to join the John Player team. There was such a shortage of good bikes it was Hobson's choice really, and I joined them for the 1973 season. Now Peter Williams was a very good rider, and one of the reasons I know this is that twin-cylinder Norton he was plugging away on for years was the biggest load of crap out.

How bad was it? Well, I can remember riding the thing at Daytona at the beginning of 1973 and a 250, misfiring, passed me going down the straight. That's how slow they were. I rode the John Player Norton a few times but it was never a truly competitive motorbike. It looked smart and it had a modern monocoque frame, but mechanically it was old and unreliable.

Another reason I decided to join the team was that Phil Read left it. I said at the time: "I like being popular. If I was as popular as Phil Read I'd stop tomorrow. The two of us couldn't possibly be in the same team. How could a team manage with a hard-headed bloke like me riding alongside such a nice lad like Phil?"

I went to South Africa with Frank and the team and at the circuit at Pietermaritzburg it was about 100 degrees, absolutely baking hot. Peter in all his wisdom had designed the bike and he'd got this bloody great fairing completely enclosing the engine. And it was an air-cooled engine! There were no vents in the front of the fairing at all and I said: "Let's cut the fairing off at the front, let some heat out." He wouldn't let me. "Oh no," he said, "it's all been worked out and air is being routed where it's needed. We mustn't touch the fairing." Rubbish! I was leading the 750 race and the engine and gearbox got that ruddy hot the gearbox melted and it got stuck in top gear. Race over.

Then we went to Kyalami and I was going round in an open practice where

Aboard the John Player Norton in the Match Races at Mallory Park
(Nick Nicholls Collection, Mortons Archive)

cars and bikes were out together. I was in between two Minis going through a 100mph-plus left-hand bend when the Mini in front broke a con-rod and dropped oil on the track. When my tyres hit the oil the steering went all funny as you might expect. I got into a massive slide and then I got chucked off. I tumbled over and over and bounced down the track.

It was ages before I slid to a stop but when I did, the chap who had been behind me and saw it all unfold ran across and picked me up. He said: "I've never seen anything like that. I'm so pleased to see you're all right, I thought you'd be dead." Then he came to see me later on in the paddock and he said: "I've just been working it out. You were travelling at 130ft a second when you were bouncing down the road."

After that I rode the Norton at Rouen, which was a street circuit in France. This time the primary chain broke and I got chucked off once again. I smashed my glasses and bashed my face in. I was concussed and black and blue from head to foot. The medics wanted me to go to hospital but I refused and came home in the John Player lorry. Next was Brands Hatch and the bike was hopelessly outpaced once more. I told the team manager, Frank Perris, I was wasting my time and the Norton was not as fast as my 350 Yamsel. In fact, I told him the transporter was faster.

MORE STORIES

Ray Pickrell was a really nice bloke. I liked Ray a lot and when he fell off at Mallory Park and suffered a serious injury which ended up finishing his career I wanted to do something to help him get back on his feet. He was in hospital in Leicester after the accident so I went to see him. I'd won three races the day he got hurt, pulling in something like £1000 so I gave it all to Ray to help during his rehabilitation. Guess what he did? He bought his dad a car! I thought: "Bloody hell, that's not what I had in mind." But then again perhaps that was where the money was most needed.

When I rode the John Player Norton at Imola in 1973 it was snowing and old man Costa said practising was postponed until the next day. So Mike Hailwood sent someone off to get some booze and we were all sitting around enjoying a drink and a chat when the sun came out and the snow melted away. Costa said: "Right, come on everyone, practice is back on, out you go." But Mike said: "No we're bloody well not, we're all half pissed!"

It was at Imola that Peter Williams' missus, Carrie, was sitting on a camping chair in their awning when a helicopter came incredibly low over the paddock. The awning got sucked up and Carrie was pulled up with it until she was about 10ft in the air. The helicopter landed nearby and someone's mechanic stormed over to it, opened the door while the blades were still going round, and whack! He thumped the pilot in the mouth. And it was at Imola once more that Peter Williams set off in the paddock in his van, dragging his bikes along on their sides behind it, completely forgetting he'd tied them down and looped the rope around his tow bar.

At Cadwell Park one year a young guy called Mick Grant came to my attention. He had dirty scruffy leathers, a scruffy red beard, a scruffy bike, and a scruffy van which he'd parked on uneven ground in the worst part of the paddock. Ruddy puddles all around. But I noticed he wasn't a bad rider. I went to see him and I said: "Let me give you some advice, Mick. Get yourself some nice new leathers, have a bloody good shave, clean your van up, and park somewhere on the level. If you do all that I'll help you out and get you a pair of decent bikes."

Anyway, he took my advice and I sorted him out with a couple of Yamahas. But then he rang me up and said: "I can't go ahead with the arrangement because I'm going to ride for Padgetts." I said: "That's no problem, Mick. I'll keep the bikes and get them ready to go because when you fall out with the Padgett brothers they'll be here for you."

About three months went by and sure enough he came to me and said: "Have you still got those bikes, John?" I said: "This is the deal. Take the bikes and give me 50% of the prize money you win. When you've paid enough to buy the bikes, they're yours to keep." I sold them to him on these easy terms with all the spares he needed and for a very cheap price. It helped him get established and put him on the road to success. And I put a word in later on to help him get his Kawasaki ride as well.

PETER WILLIAMS

Road racer, race bike designer and mechanical engineer

In the early Sixties, before I started racing, it seemed to me that John Cooper was winning everything. Before that it was Mike Hailwood. That was my impression. He was top of the heap and if I were to go through the results I'd be sure to find John in first place much of the time. It was either Mike Hailwood, Derek Minter or John Cooper and that's about it. He was a very good rider indeed and greatly respected. You've got to respect the guy who's winning the races!

He started racing some years before I did and my first contact with John was at Scarborough in 1964. Although I was a new rider – what today would be called a rookie – I somehow put in the fastest lap in practice. It was my first time there on my own bikes and he was an established winner and very good at Scarborough. Before the race he said to me: "Be careful under the trees because it's slippery there." I thought: "Oh yeah?"

Was he trying to help me? I don't know. I think he was trying to get into my head, psychological stuff. But I really don't know. In the race I overtook him going down the long straight, and here we see an example of him being savvy where I wasn't. I was new and green and I overtook him on the bumpy side of the road so when I put the brakes on they locked and I fell off. John went on to win. I shouldn't have been in that position. I shouldn't have been trying to overtake the established winner at Scarborough. I was inexperienced and I was lucky to get away without any injuries.

John Cooper is somebody with innate intelligence. He's not a highly educated bloke but he's clever, he's shrewd, and he sees where the best chance is. He makes good judgments and as a motorbike racer he was an absolute natural. He had an innate ability. Where that comes from who knows, but he was an extremely good motorcycle rider. As a rider and as a person he has this natural savvy.

Saying that, I think one does have to work hard to become a good rider, or good at anything. I don't know about John but I used to sit in the van before a race and imagine myself going round the circuit and even in the winter I used to envisage myself riding a motorbike. Sitting in a chair, doing that and then getting up at the end of it with sweaty hands. I don't know about John's methods but whatever he did, it worked. He was a very good rider indeed.

He had his own style and his own ways of doing things which were highly successful. I raced against John quite often over the years. He had this knee-out riding style, climbing all over the bike, which I didn't and couldn't do.

But it obviously worked well for him. He was a racer, that was the point about John. He was one of those people who wanted to win. He wasn't there to come second and more often than not he didn't have to deal with being beaten because he did win.

Another memory of John from early in my career was when I managed to get into the Race of the Year at Mallory Park as the last qualifier. I was on a slow bike and in the race John lapped me, but he passed me into a bend in such a way that I suddenly saw what made him go so quick. That was a great lesson for me.

In those days there was a saying: slow in, fast out. Go into a bend relatively slowly and come out quick, but what John was doing – and I subsequently worked on it very hard – was fast in, fast out. When he overtook me at Mallory Park he gave me a perfect demonstration of his technique. You trail-brake into the corner. There's an awful lot of talk about how best to do it even now. It is remarkable that a skilled rider can judge within a fraction of a second how to take a bend properly, perfectly and extremely quickly. It's a remarkable thing for a human being to do and I think John was able to do it better than anybody else at the time.

There was absolutely no problem being wheel to wheel with John. He was a safe rider and he never pushed or barged or behaved badly in any way, but then we didn't in those days. It wasn't worth it. There were one or two that did but they would usually come unstuck.

In those days if you took a liberty and suffered for it, or, worse, made somebody else suffer for it, forever would the consequences be felt. The sufferers would really suffer because if you crashed in those days it was likely you would die or be extremely seriously injured. Nowadays, with body armour and today's race track design, the likelihood is you will walk away. If you're unlucky you might break something. Only very rarely is there a fatality.

But in those days death was much more likely so we didn't mess about and if someone a bit wild came along we'd sort things out among ourselves. Racing was much cleaner.

Another story about John – and this time I came out on top. By now I was well established and we were at Oulton Park. He was a man to beat there but so was I and he said to me: "The prize for first place this afternoon is £100 and an Omega watch. If you and I find ourselves in the lead, let me come first and I'll give you the £100 because I'd really like the watch." I thought: "Eff you, I'll have both!" Well, I did win and I got the Omega watch and the £100 but he probably got 300% more start money than I did that day – so he did okay!

Why did John not get a factory ride? Thinking about it now, I think John and I were similar in nature in this respect. We thought if you did well enough, the bloke with the big cigar would eventually come along and give you the works ride you deserved. But that wasn't enough. You had to be obsequious, go around hugging people, buttering them up, sucking up to them. Absolutely the last thing John would ever do!

We were team-mates briefly and I know John does have a bit of a go at me about the Norton I designed because I was keen to make sure that only the air that caught the engine would go into the cooling ducts on the front of the bike.

I didn't like the idea of air going into the duct to no good purpose, creating drain. He said you could spit on the crankcase and it would sizzle. Well, I used to think: "Yes John, but it's a heat engine. That's what it is, it gets hot."

I think the Norton went very well for what it was and it makes me uncomfortable to think about John criticising my engineering which I feel was actually quite successful in many ways.

But John Cooper is a really good bloke, a decent man whom I respect. He was a superb rider who could ride absolutely anything. A bloody great Triumph, a little 250, and his Seeley Yamaha all in the same meeting. And earlier in his career he started off by winning on really small bikes.

And I owe him a vote of thanks because in many ways, right at the start of my own racing career, John Cooper taught me how to ride a bike.

Cooper (BSA) and Read (Norton), Brands Hatch, Easter 1972 (Jan Burgers)

The 1972 Formula 750 TT was a disaster for the John Player Norton team. All three riders failed to finish, with gearbox troubles putting John and Phil Read out on the first lap (Motopix)

That Cooper style. Hutchinson 100, Brands Hatch, 1972

John shows Cal Rayborn (Harley-Davidson) and Dick Mann (BSA) the way at Oulton Park in April 1972. Peter Williams brings up the rear (Nick Nicholls Collection, Mortons Archive)

John Cooper leads Dave Aldana, Anglo-American Match Races, Brands Hatch, Easter 1973 (Nick Nicholls Colection, Mortons Archive)

Blast off at Mallory Park, race winner Jarno Saarinen is to John's left (Malcolm Carling Collection)

Leading Chas Mortimer at Tilburg, Netherlands, 1972
(Jan Burgers)

Still fast! Cooperman on the BSA
(Motopix)

At Brands Hatch on the BSA triple
(Mortons Archive)

RETIREMENT

Chris Carter: So you gave up on the John Player Norton and not long after that you retired from the sport. What brought that about?

Later on in 1973 I was back on a BSA when I crashed at Brands Hatch in an MCN Superbikes round. Going down the hill I fell off and hit the bank that's not there any more and I broke the tibia and fibia in my right leg.

The next day I was lying in hospital at Dartford with my leg in a pot and I came to thinking perhaps it was time to chuck it in. I'd got the garage to run and racing was always a bit nerve-racking. You'd wake up on a Sunday morning with your stomach turning over and I suddenly felt I'd had enough of it all.

I'd started racing when I was 16 so I'd been at it a good few years. Besides, I was going to be six months or more in a plaster cast so the current season would be well and truly over by the time I could get back on a bike.

I wondered if it wasn't worth starting again after that, besides which I'd got no competitive bikes.

At that time there was a serious shortage of good machinery. BSA had packed up completely by then so there was no factory support or development. The bike I'd been riding at Brands was privately entered and two years on from the Race of the Year it had become outclassed.

After mulling it over thoroughly I decided enough was enough and I announced that I'd retired.

Chris Carter: And you were never tempted to reverse that decision and make a comeback? You were only 35.

Several times over the next few years I was asked to come back and ride again but I'd decided and that was it. I'd had a good career but it was over. It was time to call it a day.

Catching up with Jack Findlay soon after retirement
(Jan Burgers)

INJURIES

Chris Carter: The broken leg was obviously a bad one, but is it fair to say you were fairly lucky with injuries overall over the years?

I had a few injuries but when I think about it I was unbelievably lucky. I didn't do too bad really. Apart from breaking my right leg at Brands Hatch when I finished, I broke my collarbone, fractured my skull, cut an eyelid and got concussed a couple of times. I fetched a kneecap off once but got that stuck back on. Nothing too serious!

I broke a finger at Oulton Park when I fell off my Yamsel and the first aiders wanted to take me to Chester Hospital. I said: "That's no good. I've got to ride again tomorrow. Can you straighten it up for me?"

They weren't much help so I made a splint, taped it round and won a race the next day. In another accident at Oulton Park I broke my collarbone and again I didn't want to go to the hospital.

I took myself to Derby Royal Infirmary later on and on the way there I had a minor bump in the car. Ooh, my collarbone didn't half hurt then.

On the grass!
Moon Eyes on the mower
(Mortons Archive)

HOME LIFE

An impressive trophy cabinet
(John Cooper Collection)

Chris Carter: **Tell us a little about your personal life outside of racing.**

My first wife, Barbara, died tragically young of a brain tumour. We had a daughter, Jane, who was born in 1961 and when Barbara died, my mother looked after Jane for a number of years.

Later I used to date a girl called Helen who worked at E W Bliss in Derby and we ended up living together. I was going to race in South Africa when I was living with Helen and I went to see Arthur Taylor, who was the clerk of the course at Mallory Park and a solicitor's clerk by profession. I told him I wanted to make a will. He said: "The best thing you can do is marry Helen." Well, I did that and we had a daughter, Judith. But then sadly things went wrong and one night she said: "I'm going to get divorced," which shook me up, I can tell you.

That divorce cost me an awful lot of money. I lost almost everything and had to start again. I was sleeping in a caravan in the back yard at work for ages until I got back on my feet. Arthur felt ever so guilty about what happened and when he died he left me some money in his will! Arthur could be a difficult man.

He wasn't easy to like and he didn't have many friends, but he was basically all right. When he was old I used to drive him around when he wasn't feeling well, and go round to see him at night and take him a bottle of whisky. I honestly didn't think he had any savings at all and when he died I was shocked to receive the money.

After my divorce I decided I wasn't going to have any more to do with relationships with women because I didn't seem to be very good at it. But that's not how it turned out and I was a bit fortunate in the end because I ended up marrying a rich widow. I tell her that!

I knew Rosemary's first husband actually, and I knew Rosemary a little bit because she used to come into my garage for petrol. Our GP, Dr Blackwell, was a mutual friend and one day he asked me if I'd join him and his wife, with Rosemary, for dinner. Then he cancelled, saying I'd have to take her on my own. We got on well and it went from there. We've been together for 40 years now and married for 25. She's a bit bossy, like women are, but in a good way. Just the job!

My daughter Jane lives opposite us and it's good to have her near. Her first husband died and she had a tough time of it, but then a house came up for sale opposite where Rosemary and I live. It hadn't been lived in for 20 years and was in a poor state but we built a new one on the site. She lives there now with her husband Nigel. I have two grandchildren. Eleanor is a staff nurse at the Royal Derby Hospital and Edward is serving in the Royal Navy, and I'm very proud of them both.

BURGLARY

Chris Carter: **I remember back in the 1990s a lot of valuable bikes were stolen from your works premises. What happened, and did you ever get any of them back?**

I had six bikes stolen in a burglary at my garage including a Geoff Barry 500cc G50 Matchless, the Norton I won the Race of the Year on in 1965, my Yamsel, Norman Storer's speedway bike and a Yamaha TY80 child's trials bike. They were all immaculate and in perfect working order and losing the Yamsel was particularly heartbreaking.

I'd gone to America for a wedding and while I was over there the whole lot were stolen. I kept the bikes upstairs and the place was heavily alarmed. There was a lift we used to take bikes up and down and the bar which disabled it was stored elsewhere in the building. The thieves somehow knew where the bar was and how to get the lift working, and the burglar alarm was somehow burnt out and disabled without it going off. This meant they could get all the bikes down in the lift without deafening klaxons going off all the time and attracting attention. It was all very suspicious indeed.

Barry Sheene kindly offered a reward of £5000 for information and I matched it, but we never heard anything and the police did nothing about it. The insurance company paid me a fair price in the end but I'd rather have had the bikes back. I don't know what's happened to them, they've all disappeared without trace and to my knowledge they've never surfaced anywhere. Obviously, they're worth less stripped down for parts but that's probably what's happened. In fact, I was very lucky my 500 Seeley wasn't stolen as well because it was on display at an exhibition in London at the time.

'Nice to see you again Mike!' With Mike Hailwood in 1978 (Unknown)

THE BEST OF ALL TIME

Chris Carter: Who do you think was the greatest ever motorcycle racer?

Because I've been around racing a long time, people inevitably ask me who was the best of all time. Geoff Duke? John Surtees? Mike Hailwood? Kenny Roberts? Valentino Rossi? I've seen them all in action and raced against a good few of them. Well you can't compare eras, but all these top riders had very good bikes when they were at the top so they were bound to get good results.

Now Giacomo Agostini won 15 world championships and of course he was a very good rider indeed, absolutely brilliant, and he beat some good people. But when he won many of his championships he was riding against Nortons and Matchlesses and his MVs were 25mph quicker than anybody else's bike. Some years it was just ridiculous. Much is made of comparing Ago's career results with those of Valentino Rossi, but at times during Rossi's career he's been up against very tough opposition.

When I was riding in the 1960s we'd ride 250cc, 350cc and 500cc machines in the same day, but nowadays people say oh no, you can't do that. Mike Hailwood was something special. I've seen Hailwood ride three classes in a day at a grand prix and win them all. Freddie Spencer won world championships in two classes in the same year of course, but there's been no one since. I went out for dinner with him recently and I asked him if he thought it could still be done. He said of course it could, if someone really wanted to.

But nowadays I think sometimes the riders are too fussy. I know things have changed but I can remember Mike Hailwood riding that 500 Honda of his and winning races on it and I can tell you from first-hand experience, riding it at Snetterton and Oulton Park, it was an absolute pig and a half to ride. Unbelievable! It scared me and how he managed to win on it I just do not know.

Chris Carter: What are your thoughts on the current crop of riders and on the sport today? Do you think you would be competitive if you were riding now?

I think working on my bikes helped me as a rider. I know riders today who don't know anything about the bikes they're riding. They never get their hands dirty. And when riders fall off these days they just walk away. When I was riding you had to pick your bike up, push it back to the paddock and get the spanners out and repair it. These days when they come in after practice they jump straight off and go and sit in a chair while everything's taken care of and someone sits down with him and takes notes while he talks about every little wobble.

And it amazes me that a rider wins a grand prix, then the next week in practice he's nowhere on the time sheets... saying the bike won't steer, and this, that and the other is wrong with it. People are on the phone to Japan or Bologna and the mechanics are all looking at the computers and scratching their heads. Another thing, of course, is it's prohibitively expensive now. Not just the bikes but tyres and fuel and the entry fees.

But of course, riders like Lorenzo and Rossi and Crutchlow are fantastic and unbelievably brave. Would I be able to ride like them? I don't honestly know. I remember a few years after I retired, I was talking to Barry Sheene and I said I didn't know if I could have adapted to using the huge fat slicks he was running on his Suzuki at the time. He said: "You'd be fine. Change is gradual and you get used to things step by step." I guess he was right, you don't go straight from a Manx Norton to a 200bhp MotoGP Yamaha or Honda, so yes, I guess I'd cope. The bikes gradually get better, and whatever era you're riding in, you gradually get better with them.

Today's riders have come through Moto3 and Moto2. They haven't just jumped straight on to MotoGP machines.

Another thing I disagree with is that nowadays there's the British Superbikes, World Superbikes and MotoGP and each series has the same line-up week after week, month after month, and pretty much year after year. The same riders at the same tracks. Following the Formula One model has meant everything's signed up at the start of the season with the same riders on the grid for each race and nobody else gets a chance to get into it. Well, years ago more people got an opportunity to have a go against the top stars on the continent. And in Britain there used to be events like the Race of the Year at Mallory Park and the Race of Aces at Snetterton, where world champions such as John Surtees and Mike Hailwood would be in the field. And at places like Cadwell Park and Scarborough, top foreign stars like Jarno Saarinen and Ago would be in the programme. I remember in 1970, Ago turned up to race at Cadwell the same day the Spanish Grand Prix was on, because he'd already wrapped up the 350 and 500 world titles. Incredible when you think about it, and great for the fans.

Sharing a joke with Chris Carter and Percy Tait before fast-parading in 1982
(Mortons Archive)

JULIAN RYDER
Motorcycling journalist and broadcaster

John Cooper's racing career was a little bit before my time and although I will have seen him in action when I very first started going as a fan, I wouldn't have known what I was looking at! I'm not a historian of his period but I admire him immensely.

You've only got to look at the record books to see what he did on all sorts of tracks around the world. He was a short-circuit man but he also competed at the top level in 500cc grands prix racing, getting on the podium with Hailwood and Agostini at the absolute top of the sport. That alone makes him a fast racer in anybody's language. And when Mike came home to race in the UK, John would give him a run for his money and sometimes beat him. No question at all, John Cooper was very, very quick.

Over the years I've got to know John personally over a beer here and there and I like him a lot. He's still well connected and got his ear very much to the ground, and he knows exactly what's going on. He's always been very helpful to me when I've needed some information for a story. But more than that, he's a typical old racer from that period. He's funny, he's full of stories and while he's an absolute gentleman it's clear he was a tough specimen in his time. After all, he rode in a tough era full of tough guys.

The British scene was intensely competitive with a busy calendar. He was one of the top men. Minter, Degens, and a great many others, all tough men and difficult to beat and they spent a lot of time beating one another. Derek Minter was virtually impossible to beat at Brands Hatch at times but most of the time you'd turn up as a spectator and really not know who of maybe 10 riders was going to win. John was one of those men slugging it out every weekend and he probably won more often than anyone.

His time was right on the cusp between what might be called the classic era and the modern era. Dr Martin Raines, the official MotoGP statistician, always refers to 1974 as the start of the modern era in grands prix, whether that's because the RG500 turned up, or there were more reliable statistics or because of the organisation of the championship, I'm not sure.

If you look at his grand prix record in the top class he was nobody's mug and in 1968 he was eighth in the championship on his own Seeley, even though he only did two or three rounds. It just wasn't financially worthwhile for guys like John to do a full grand prix season. You certainly didn't make money out of racing in grands prix because the organisers knew you wanted to race there and they were distinctly ungenerous with their dealing.

And what 500cc works rides were there in the late 1960s apart from on the MV Agusta? Answer: none. Those seats were taken and there were not enough places in the other classes either for all the talented racers, one of whom was definitely John. Was he good enough? Of course he was.

One-off international meetings were more lucrative for John than grands prix and, later on, riding the BSA triple probably earned him some decent money. He had a fantastic final flourish with the BSA triple which I hope will have been a good earner for him. They were big-haul races. Big crowds and strong entries with good prize money. And of course John was always clever with his money. He didn't waste it and he invested it in his garage and other businesses.

He had a very noticeable riding style. Theatrical, knee out, hanging off. Whether he invented it or not is another matter, but he was definitely one of the pioneers. You've only got to look at photographs from the time to see that John was ahead of his time, not just in riding with his knees out but in shifting his bodyweight around rather than sitting neatly and precisely on the centreline of the bike in the way John Surtees or Geoff Duke did.

It makes sense that John worked out there was something to be had by adopting this riding technique both in machine control and carburettor draught. And you know what racers are like, he didn't share that information with people, he probably thought he could grab an advantage.

Would John be competitive today? Daft question. If you were fast in the Sixties, you'd be fast in 2020. Riding technique is an irrelevant argument. If a guy has it in him to go fast on a racing motorcycle it doesn't matter what era you drop him in, he will be fast.

It's ridiculous to try to freeze a rider's style in time. If John has any personal doubts about this, for once I'll say he is wrong.

ARTWORK: TED

Up, up and away. John Cooper about to take to the air (Mortons Archive)

Chocks away. John about to fly with the Red Arrows (Cooper Collection)

FLYING

Chris Carter: Flying was a hobby of yours for many years. A lot of racers seem drawn to it. Is it as difficult as it looks?

I flew light aeroplanes for quite a few years. It was a challenge. Something to do that meant using my brains a bit learning to fly the plane, carrying out the procedures, reading a map, working out times. I used to fly back and forth to Brands Hatch and Snetterton, and occasionally over to the Isle of Man. It was quite handy.

To get a basic pilot's licence isn't actually all that difficult. I used to fly VFR – visual flight rules. I always flew where I could see where I was going and I was never very keen on cloudy conditions. To fly in cloud you have to follow IFR – instrument flight rules – and to do that properly you've got to do a lot of it and get familiar with it.

To be a commercial pilot or a helicopter pilot you've got to be completely switched on. Very bright indeed. A pal of mine, Stuart, has just retired after doing 25,000 hours on airlines flying all types of aircraft. He'd turn up for work not knowing where he'd be going that day. It could be the Czech Republic or Tenerife and no matter what the weather was he could cope with it.

And if you said to him you've got 100 litres of fuel, how many gallons is that, and what's the weight of it, he'd tell you straight away. And if you said to him you're going down a track at one-eight-zero and you go for 27 miles and the wind's at two-seven-zero 10 knots, how far will you be off course at the end, he'd tell you that too. I couldn't do that sort of thing.

I never owned a plane. Renting an aeroplane cost a lot less than buying one. Someone I know had a big boat. It cost him about a million and a half quid. I asked him if it was expensive to run and he said: "Just imagine getting a giant sack, filling it with £50 notes and chucking it over the side every year. That's the cost of running a boat." Nowadays owning and running a Cessna 172 plane would work out at around £250 an hour and it's only £175 an hour to hire one.

Visiting the Red Arrows
(Cooper Collection)

Chris Carter: I know you've flown with the Red Arrows. That's quite something.

I was very friendly with the Red Arrows for a while. I flew with them in a Gnat with my pal Jon Tye, who was a very experienced pilot and chief flying instructor who flew Jet Provosts and all sorts of things including Vulcans for many years. Jon flew with the Red Arrows a lot and he had a good mate, Ken Tate, who was in the team.

Dicky Duckett was the leader of the Arrows. He used to fly Vulcans and he knew Jon. He rang him up one day and said: "It's my last year with the team. Do you want to have a fly with us before I finish?" Jon said: "Great, I'd love to. Can I bring a mate of mine?" So he took me down there and I flew in a two-seater Gnat on a full display. Through flying I got to know the Stevenson brothers, who owned the Commodore Hotel in Nottingham. They asked me if I'd mind picking the TV presenter Keith Chegwin up from Alton Towers and taking him to meet them at Tollerton Airfield. From there they were going to fly him down to Kent for a live show somewhere near Dover.

I was pleased to help and I went along to keep Keith company during the flight. When we got in the aeroplane, one of the Stevenson brothers said: "There's some whisky there in the back if you want to help yourselves." Big mistake. We knocked it back and polished off the entire bottle, although of course Cheggers drank far more than me, and when we got to Dover he could hardly stand up. "What have you done to him?" said the guy picking him up. "He's on stage in a couple of hours."

Of course none of us had any idea about Keith's drink problems. I really enjoyed his company. He was a really smashing bloke and it was a terrible shame he died so young.

'Listen to what I'm telling you, Barry!' John always got on very well with Barry Sheene
(Mortons Archive)

BARRY SHEENE

Barry Sheene: 'Coop taught me a lot about what it took to get to the top in the sport.'

Chris Carter: It's no secret Barry Sheene and I didn't always see eye to eye, but you and Barry were always quite close despite there being a 12-year age gap between you. Tell us about your friendship with Barry over the years.

I'm not sure exactly how he saw me, whether an older brother or father figure or just a mate, but Barry Sheene and I always got on really well. In his later years we were always talking together on the phone and I helped him as a young man and he rode my Yamsel once or twice, but then again I helped a lot of riders. We just got on.

When people helped him he always appreciated it, but I will say he used to try to stop other people getting works Suzukis that were as quick as his, people like Randy Mamola, Pat Hennen, John Newbold and one or two others. But he wasn't the only one who has done that sort of thing over the years and it still happens now.

There was an occasion in the 1980s when he was injured and he made sure Roger Burnett got his bike and not Rob McElnea because he didn't see Roger as such a threat. Barry said to him: "The bike's so quick you'll win easy but don't make it obvious, just creep by them. And afterwards just say you've won it because the bike's so beautifully prepared and nice to ride." Roger said the bike was the fastest thing he'd ever ridden. Absolutely unbelievably quick.

Before the 1971 Race of the Year I told young Barry to be very careful because Ago and I would be going a lot faster than he did against him in the 500 race earlier on. I said: "We'll be a second a lap faster than you so don't overdo it trying to keep up." But when I came round Gerards Bend on the third lap there was Barry in the ruddy ditch. Later on I said: "What did I tell you Barry?" He said: "My footrest caught on the ground." I said: "Yes lad, they tend to do that when you fall off."

When he lived in Wisbech in Cambridgeshire he rang me up and said he wanted a new Rolls-Royce. I said: "You're in luck. Remember the chap who owns the restaurant where we went out to dinner last time you were up here, Joe Waldron? He wants to sell his Roller." "Well," he said, "can you bring it down for me?" So I did and Rosemary fetched me back.

Another time he rang me up from his house in Surrey and said: "I'm racing at Donington tomorrow and I've got this bloody terrible toothache. I'm coming up this afternoon in my helicopter. Do you know a dentist in your area?" I told him no problem. I had a friend called Stuart who was a dentist so I rang him and fixed things up, then when Barry flew in I picked him up and took him to see Stuart.

While he was working on Barry's tooth Stuart said: "Barry, your throat is so inflamed I can't believe it. It's going to give you serious trouble eventually. You must stop smoking now." He smoked 60 Gauloises a day at the time. Ripped the tips off and smoked them backwards. Of course he didn't listen.

When Barry and Stephanie moved down under he rang me up one day and he said: "We're coming over from Australia, will

1 8 9 8
MATINIC
ADVENTUR
SUZUKI
SUZUKI
750

32

John Cooper holds a watching brief behind Barry Sheene, Guyla Marsovszky, Jarno Saarinen and Rod Gould, Silverstone, August, 1971. Barry won the race
(Malcolm Carling Collection)

you come down to London and stop at the Conrad Hotel with us, I can get you a special deal." It was a great deal: £250 a night down from £450, and that night we went for a meal with Stephanie and her sister, who was a TV presenter. And when we left the restaurant and went into the bar Gloria Hunniford was there. Stephanie knew her so we all sat together for an hour or so and she was a charming woman, absolutely lovely.

I've met a lot of famous men and women through racing and most of them were nice people. I used to knock about with Colin Crompton of the Wheeltappers and Shunters and through him I met a lot of well-known characters such as Bernard Manning and Les Dawson. Les Dawson was a lovely man and great fun to be with, Rosemary liked him a lot. Bernard Manning was nice enough too actually, but I couldn't possibly repeat most of the things he said in mixed company, it was so packed with expletives! Princess Anne, Michael Bentine, Henry Cooper, Raymond Baxter, Murray Walker and Richard Stilgoe also come to mind as very pleasant people. And Barry Sheene was big mates with George Harrison of the Beatles.

One year when we had a hospitality suite at Donington Park, George Harrison came to the door. Rosemary didn't recognise him and said: "Sorry, this is a private party," and she sent him on his way. A bit later I realised what had happened and went off looking for him. I found him chatting with Tom Wheatcroft and Barry Sheene. "I'm really sorry George," I said. "Oh don't worry, it's all right," he said. He was fine about it.

Barry badgered us to go out and stay with him in Australia. He went on and on about it and eventually I said to Rosemary: "Okay, let's go." When we arrived at his house it was late and when Barry showed us our room, he said: "When Steph asks you what you want for your breakfast tomorrow tell her you want a full English – egg, bacon, sausage, the works." Sure enough we went downstairs in the morning and she said: "Right you two, what do you want for breakfast?" I answered as instructed and she said: "Well you can eff off down the cafe if that's what you want. I'm not getting my pans and cooker filthy dirty doing that."

Steph is really fussy and fanatical about cleanliness, She keeps her home absolutely immaculate and her kitchen sparkling clean. Of course, Barry had set me up, and he was standing in the background chuckling away. We had a great time with Barry and Stephanie in Australia and enjoyed getting to know their kids, Freddie and Sidonie. Freddie got on particularly well with Rosemary, diving in the swimming pool with her every day and having fun in the sun.

Rosemary got on very well indeed with Stephanie Sheene, and she told her a few tales. When Barry was racing at the British Grand Prix at Silverstone they always stayed with Lord and Lady Hesketh in their stately home nearby at Easton Neston.

The first night they were there they always had a posh dinner party but despite his race team and flamboyant lifestyle it seems Lord Hesketh was not always a big spender. When the roast beef or whatever would appear and be set on the table, Steph said Barry was always aghast. He would groan and say to her he could eat the entire piece of meat himself but he had to sit and watch while it was divided among 12 of them. The facilities at Easton Neston were rather limited. Apparently Stephanie once said: "Do you think I could borrow your washing machine? We've come straight from two grands prix and I need some clean clothes." "Oh," said Lady Hesketh, "I don't know if we've got a washing machine."

So she called for the housekeeper who said to Stephanie: "Come with me and I'll show you what we've got." So the housekeeper took her down to the cellars where there was an old twin tub. Stephanie said: "I'm not sure I even know how to use one of those." The housekeeper said: "I'm sorry but the only alternative is to soak everything in the bath." Stephanie said to the Heskeths later: "Why don't you buy that poor woman a decent washing machine?"

Well, the following year the housekeeper greeted them warmly. "Ooh Mrs Sheene," she said, "I do want to thank you. Since you were last here we've got a brand new washing machine and a tumble dryer as well!"

Many years later, in 2002, Barry was scheduled to ride at a big classic festival at Donington Park. He rang me from Australia and said: "I want you and Rosemary to come to dinner with me at Donington Manor on the Thursday, Friday and Saturday nights." That seemed a bit odd. I said: "We'll come on one night, why don't you invite some other friends on other nights?" But he was insistent. "No," he said. "I want you and Rosemary to be with me each night. I'll cover the bill but I want you to be there."

A long-term friendship
(Suzuki pic by John Cooke)

I noticed on the Saturday night particularly, when he had a fillet steak, that he was having trouble swallowing his food and he kept sipping water after every mouthful. I said: "What's up, Barry?" He said: "I've got a bit of a lump in my throat and I've got to see a surgeon for some test results when I get back to Australia on Tuesday."

And on the Tuesday he rang me from his home to say he'd got cancer of the oesophagus. I said: "What's the situation? Will you be having surgery?" He said: "No, I'm going to try alternative medicine and go on a a special diet." He saw specialists and went to George Harrison's clinic in Switzerland.

I rang him back a few days later and said: "I know a specialist cancer surgeon and he says he'll have a look at you and see what can be done." Again, he wouldn't consider surgery. "No," he said, "I'm dealing with this in my own way." He wouldn't consider it. Then a friend of Rosemary's who'd had successful cancer treatment told us to tell him he had to get surgery to prolong his life. I rang him once again and told him this but it was the same story, and in the end I said: "Look Barry, you know my feelings on the matter so I won't mention it again."

Not too long later his nephew Scott Smart rang me up and I said: "I think I know what you're going to tell me," and he said: "Yeah, two o'clock this morning." I don't know why Barry was so bloody awkward and refused conventional treatment. I just don't understand it. He wasn't a man who was scared of things.

CLASSIC SCENE

Chris Carter: Are you still in touch with any of the people you used to race against, and are you involved in the classic scene?

I enjoy going to classic events and I sometimes see riders from my era socially. People like Colin Seeley, Dave Croxford, Peter Williams and Dan Shorey, and it's good when we all get together. I sometimes see Dick Creith, who won the Ulster Grand Prix in 1965. He comes from Bushmills. and he and his wife are lovely people. Likewise Stuart Hicken and his wife, and Eddie Roberts. Stuart always says, anytime I want tickets for a meeting I just have to ask.

Giacomo Agostini's son is a lovely lad. He studied in England and so did his daughter. I was at a classic meeting at Scarborough a while back and Ago pointed me out to his son. "That's John Cooper," he said. "We don't speak to him. He beat me." He was just joking, of course. Ago and I get on very well.

Because I won the Race of the Year in 1971 Ago and I have been invited many times to give talks together, often for clubs or for charity, and for most of these occasions over the years I haven't received a fee. But what I didn't realise for quite some time was that while I was getting bugger all, Ago was getting quite a few Euros to turn up at these events. A few years ago I said to him: "You're a jammy sod, Ago. I won the ruddy race, but when we do these talks together you get paid to go and I get bugger all, so you've won in the end!"

It's remarkable. Those BSA triples are all over the place now. They were rare bikes but now there are loads of them! Most of them red like mine, with several described as being John Cooper's BSA. Well, they can't all be my old bikes. I've signed loads of fairings and tanks and goodness knows what else, and most of these things have had nothing directly to do with me.

It's amazing how many people still

Birthday celebrations with old racing pals and special guests Laurel and Hardy. Steve Parrish fooling around as usual

(Cooper Collection)

Racing greats and good friends, Giacomo Agostini and John Cooper

(Cooper Collection)

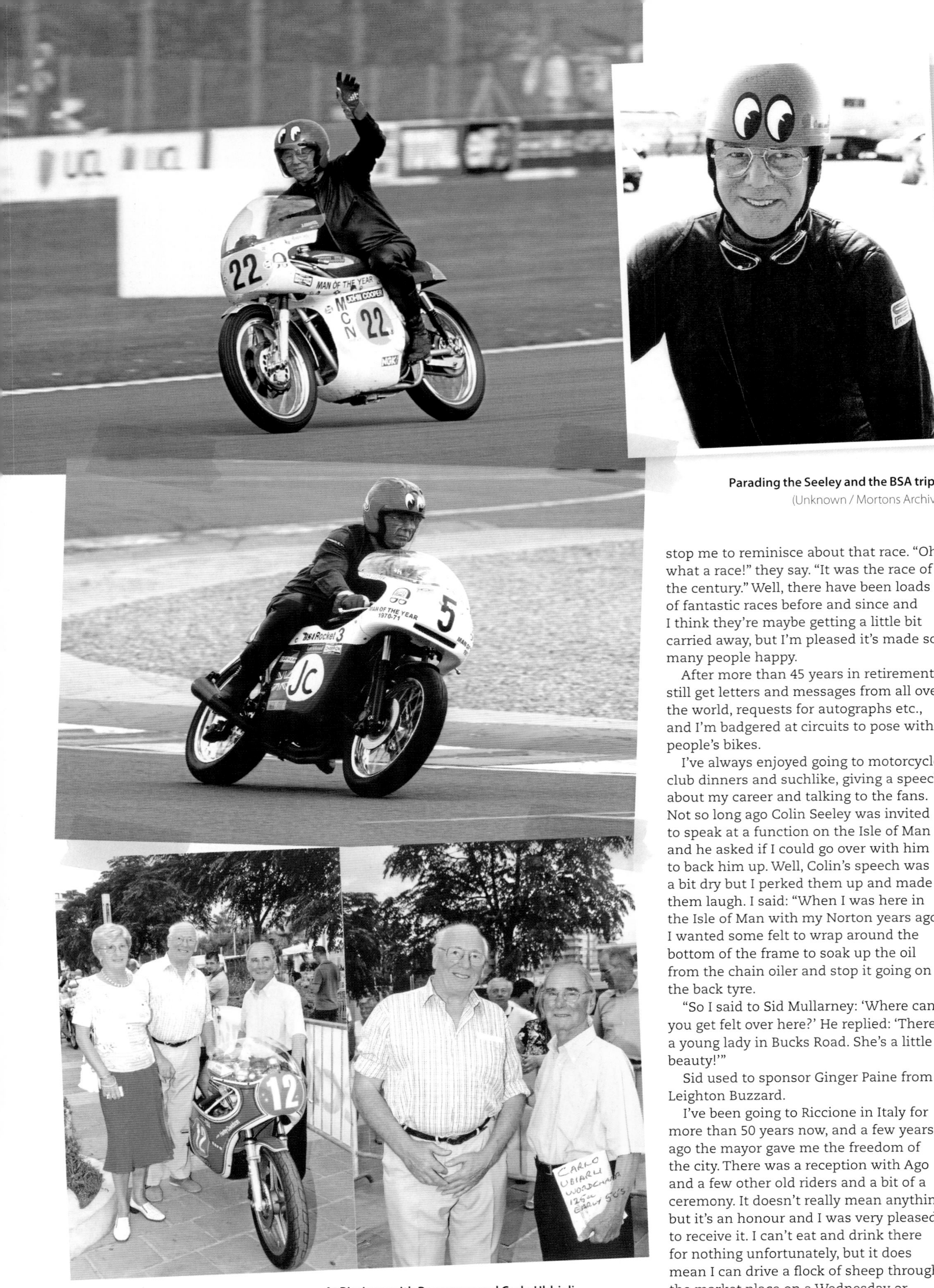

Paradina the Seeley and the BSA triple
(Unknown / Mortons Archive)

At Riccione with Rosemary and Carlo Ubbiali
(Cooper Collection)

stop me to reminisce about that race. "Oh what a race!" they say. "It was the race of the century." Well, there have been loads of fantastic races before and since and I think they're maybe getting a little bit carried away, but I'm pleased it's made so many people happy.

After more than 45 years in retirement I still get letters and messages from all over the world, requests for autographs etc., and I'm badgered at circuits to pose with people's bikes.

I've always enjoyed going to motorcycle club dinners and suchlike, giving a speech about my career and talking to the fans. Not so long ago Colin Seeley was invited to speak at a function on the Isle of Man and he asked if I could go over with him to back him up. Well, Colin's speech was a bit dry but I perked them up and made them laugh. I said: "When I was here in the Isle of Man with my Norton years ago I wanted some felt to wrap around the bottom of the frame to soak up the oil from the chain oiler and stop it going on the back tyre.

"So I said to Sid Mullarney: 'Where can you get felt over here?' He replied: 'There's a young lady in Bucks Road. She's a little beauty!'"

Sid used to sponsor Ginger Paine from Leighton Buzzard.

I've been going to Riccione in Italy for more than 50 years now, and a few years ago the mayor gave me the freedom of the city. There was a reception with Ago and a few other old riders and a bit of a ceremony. It doesn't really mean anything but it's an honour and I was very pleased to receive it. I can't eat and drink there for nothing unfortunately, but it does mean I can drive a flock of sheep through the market place on a Wednesday or something daft like that.

CHARITY

Chris Carter: I know you're involved with various charities and you always seem to be helping people out one way or another.

Money is a horrible thing really. Life revolves around it, and while it's always been important to me to make a living and pay my way, I've always tried to help others one way or another. It's wicked really that so much money goes to those who have plenty already, and that more isn't spent on the people that need it the most.

A little while back I got involved with a charity in Derby which takes underprivileged children to Skegness on holiday. My daughter teaches some of these poor kids and it's unbelievable in this day and age but some of them have never been out of Derby in their lives. I had some hats made with John Cooper Moon Eyes on them and I sold them to raise funds.

I also support the local Padley Centre for the homeless, and Rosemary and I have always backed Colin Seeley's charitable trust.

Colin asked us if there were any causes we might want his organisation to support, so on our recommendation he went to Loughborough to visit Rainbows Hospice, which helps the families of young children who are dying of cancer. Afterwards he came back to my house and cried for an hour. Colin's trust gave a considerable sum to the charity and a further amount later on.

Derek Minter was never very sociable. He always spoke but not very much, and to this day I'm not entirely sure if he was shy or a little bit arrogant. At the end of his life he had cancer and his second wife Jenny ended up with it as well. The top and bottom of it was Derek ran out of money and couldn't pay his care home costs.

I found out about this and rang the TT Riders Association in the Isle of Man. I told them Derek was in bad shape and owed some money. They paid his debt off. Then I rang Bill Smith at the ACU Benevolent Fund and told him about the situation and they paid his fees until he died.

PAT MAHONEY

Chris Carter: What about other former riders. Have you helped any former competitors? I know you were in touch with Pat Mahoney.

Pat Mahoney was a good rider and a nice bloke, but a bit militant. In the 1960s there were arguments about start money being given to some riders and not others and Pat was at the forefront of it all. I remember going to Mallory Park once and he wanted all the riders to band together and refuse to go out on to the start line. He asked me what I was getting and I said not a lot. "Well join us then," said Pat. But circuit owner Chris Lowe was threatening us with serious consequences if we took part in the strike and in the end some raced and some didn't.

I ended up feeling really sorry for Pat because he had a big accident at Brands Hatch in 1975 and he never fully recovered from it. I saw it happen. He fell off on Paddock Bend and somebody knocked him and spun him round, then somebody else hit him and spun him the other way. It was brutal and it damn near killed him. He was in a coma for a while, poor lad, and when he came out of it he was never quite right.

Actually, Pat was reasonably okay brain-wise. His sense of humour was intact, and he could understand things, but he was so physically damaged he couldn't always respond too well. He was never the same man again and because he couldn't work he was incredibly hard up.

He lived near Brands Hatch and I saw him there one day at a classic event and he didn't even have enough money to put petrol in his moped to ride home. So I bought him some petrol and I had a word with the guy from Castrol and got him some oil which we strapped to the back of his bike and off he went. And from then on I used to send him some cash each Christmas, and he always took the time to write back to thank me, which because of his injuries was obviously a painstaking thing to do and took a lot of effort.

John with old mate Pat Mahoney
(Cooper Collection)

One year I put a note in with the money saying I knew he appreciated it and he didn't have to write to thank me. But he wrote back nonetheless saying he might have been brought up in a council house, but it didn't mean he didn't have any manners!

After the accident he lived with his mother and father who looked after him, and when they grew old and died he couldn't cope any more and he shot himself. Very, very sad.

PERCY

My old mechanic Alan 'Percy' Pike also committed suicide. He seemed an unlikely candidate but his dad killed himself as well. When Percy left school he was a painter and decorator and then he came and worked for me and I took him across to the TT. He liked it so much he stayed in the Isle of Man, met a woman and married her. He was a newsagent over there.

Then for some silly reason he took his own life. There was no note but his wife said when she went out on that last morning she noticed he hadn't shaved and put his tie on, which was unusual because he always looked very smart. He said: "Cheerio Lil," and off she went.

By coincidence I phoned him up at quarter past 10 that morning and spoke to him for about 15 minutes and it seems that when he put the phone down he went off and hanged himself. When his wife came back at 12 o'clock he was hanging there, dead.

Alan 'Percy' Pike
(Cooper Collection)

SIR ROBIN MILLER

Publisher and business leader, former MCN reporter

OOps it's COOPER!

It was the MCN front page headline OOps it's COOPER which first got me hooked on John Cooper. Together with the accompanying picture of a gangly bloke on a scrambles bike, legs flailing and obviously completely out of control.

It was the mid-Sixties, I was just starting out as a reporter on Motor Cycle News and here was one of the top road racers in the country prepared to make a fool of himself on a scrambles bike.

But although John has a great sense of humour he is, in truth, absolutely nobody's fool, and over the many years since first meeting him at a road race meeting at Snetterton I have been proud to have become friends with an extremely talented and warm-hearted individual.

He helped me get a lift home from Snetterton that day having crashed my car on the way to the meeting. And I helped him to a win at a particularly wet North West 200 when things had not gone well and, sitting in his van with leathers soaked and boots full of water, he was not keen to race. I started his van to warm him up and gave a few sharp words of 'motivation'. They seemed to work.

John probably never realised his full potential on the world scene but his achievements were much greater than many of those who figured higher in world championships, and many of his triumphs will remain forever in the memories of his army of fans. His famous victory over Giacomo Agostini at the 1971 Race of the Year was quite possibly his greatest win, keeping the BSA brand alive a little longer as BSA-Triumph tried to rebuild sales through racing, even hiring Mike Hailwood for Daytona.

The Match Race series, later to be called the Transatlantic Trophy, had begun that year as a joint promotion by BSA-Triumph, who provided bikes for the American team, and Motor Circuit Developments, the owners of Brands Hatch, Mallory Park and Oulton Park. John was in the UK team on a BSA triple alongside Paul Smart and Ray Pickrell on Triumph triples, on which they had already enjoyed some success.

Came the big money events at the end of the season, in particular Mallory Park's Race of the Year, and John found himself without a competitive bike. Pleas to BSA-Triumph race shop manager Doug Hele fell on deaf ears. "We're already committed John," said Doug. "We just don't have a bike for you."

Never one to take rejection lying down and confident he had the beating not only of Messrs Smart and Pickrell but Agostini and his world championship-winning MV Agusta, John went straight to the top with a phone call to BSA-Triumph marketing boss Peter Deverall. Unwilling to overrule Hele, the response from Deverall was initially negative.

But persistence being everything, Cooper came back to him once more issuing a bold challenge: "Bring me a bike to Mallory for a test and when I break the lap record we'll talk!" A race shop spare was found and prepared and Cooper duly broke the existing lap record not once but three times. A deal was done.

The outcome was one of the most sensational and emotional short circuit races ever run on British soil with local hero John Cooper duelling the great Giacomo Agostini to a split-second defeat.

It could have been very different. As the battle intensified the crowd gasped as Cooper got the BSA completely sideways at the Esses as he pushed his tyres to the limit to stay with the Italian world champion. From my vantage point on the back straight of that amazing little circuit I, along with 60,000 others, thought he had lost it. But he roared back to the front and with a lap to go he used the torque of the 750 triple to stay ahead of the MV, accelerating through Devil's Elbow to a great and historic victory.

To the few cynics who pointed out that

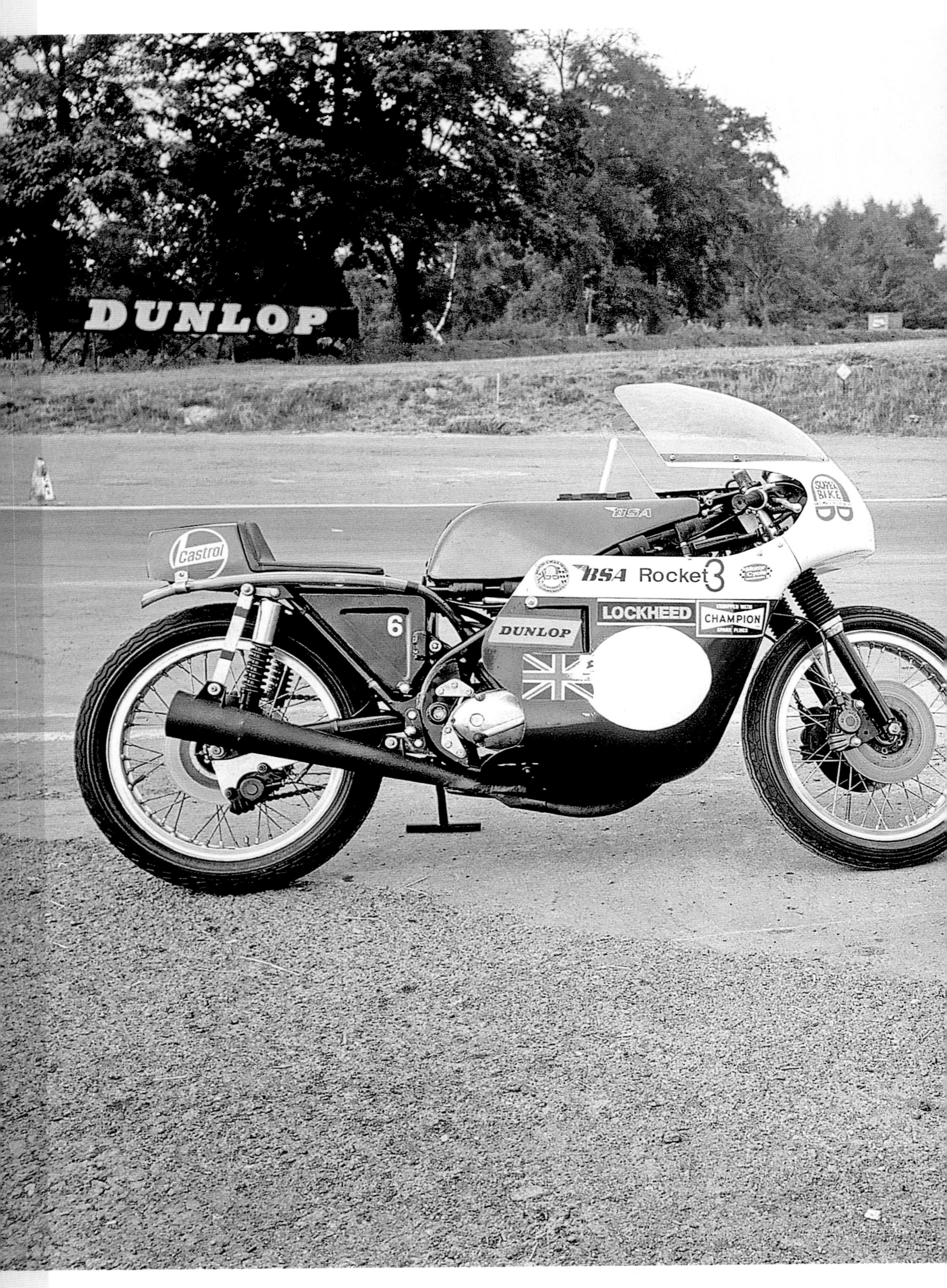
DUNLOP
BSA
Castrol
BSA Rocket3
LOCKHEED
CHAMPION
DUNLOP
6

A winning combination: John Cooper and his BSA triple
(Mortons Archive)

while Ago was on a 500 his opponent had the benefit of a 750, Cooper uttered the famous response: "It's fust under t' linen that counts."

From then John went straight on to victory at Brands Hatch, beating Ago once more, and then came the richest prize in racing, a two-leg affair at the Ontario Motor Speedway in California, US. All America's top guns were out and after a poor start Cooper had to settle for second place behind Gary Nixon in the first race. The second leg saw a huge battle between BSA-mounted Cooper and tough Australian Kel Carruthers on a 350 Yamaha. It could have been a second defeat for the English hero as, tailing the Aussie comfortably, believing there were two laps left, he belatedly saw the sign for one. Gunning the BSA hard through the last corner, he snatched victory by a tyre's width. Running up to the podium expecting to see her husband on the top step, Jan Carruthers greeted Cooper with: "You Pommie bastard!" – and then shook his hand.

As the overall winner of the event Cooper got his biggest-ever racing payout. But his $15,000 haul came in various sponsors' cheques so he had to wait around awhile in LA. And on the flight back to Blighty he found himself sitting next to a bloke who seemed to know a lot about motorbikes. Only much later did he realise he had been sitting next to Steve McQueen.

John's achievements that year caught the fans' imagination, but what the fans loved about him, and what won him the MCN Man of the Year title more than once, was not just the races he won. He was popular because he was a genuine character, and a man never afraid to speak his mind. This was great for us reporters but it didn't always go down well with the establishment such as race organisers and team sponsors, nor occasionally with other riders.

He was just different from most others. Tall, bespectacled and with a broad Derbyshire accent, he invented the knee-out riding style which together with his moon eyes helmet became his trademark. And his presence in the paddock would not go unnoticed either with helpers Bim, Jack, 'Percy' and Gordon decked in smart white overalls.

John was smart enough to invest his winnings into his businesses in Derby which have earned him a good living and provide for him in retirement. It is now many years since he raced but his love for motorbikes has never waned. He takes great pride in the classic machines in his garage, some of which he has carefully restored, and his love for riding has also not diminished. Throughout the year, in all but the foulest weather, the moon eyes helmet can still be seen out and about on the countryside roads of Derbyshire. Not bad!

John Cooper with his wife Rosemary and daughter Jane
(Cooper Collection)

MODERN LIFE

Chris Carter: Looking back, would you say you've had a good life? And how's life now you're in your ninth decade?

I'm glad I've lived the years I've lived. I'm in my eighties now and I don't like a lot of things about the way the country's run. Too many rules and regulations, huge fines for speeding, and crazy rules about health and safety.

But I still enjoy life. I go to classic events and still ride a motorbike on the road in preference to a car. I've got a sweet little Velocette and a Honda VFR. Motorcycling's been good to me and I hope I've been good for it, and that people enjoyed seeing me race. I also hope people have enjoyed reading this book.

Looking back, forgive me for repeating myself one more time but if I'd had a works bike in the late 1960s I'm certain I could have won a world championship. I proved it by breaking lap records, winning countless races including internationals, and getting on the podium in grand prix – third in Czecho when Hailwood won and Ago was second.

There was nothing special about my bike that day and Keith Huewen and Julian Ryder have said about me in their TV commentaries:

"If you can say you've stood on the podium with Giacomo Agostini and Mike Hailwood, that's quite an achievement."